my **revision** notes

Edexcel GCSE (9–1)

RELIGIOUS STUDIES: BELIEFS IN ACTION

SPECIFICATION B

Victor W. Watton

HODDER EDUCATION
AN HACHETTE UK COMPANY

In order to ensure this resource offers high-quality support for the associated Pearson qualification, it has been through a review process by the awarding body. This process confirms that this resource fully covers the teaching and learning content of the specification or part of a specification at which it is aimed. It also confirms that it demonstrates an appropriate balance between the development of subject skills, knowledge and understanding, in addition to preparation for assessment.

Endorsement does not cover any guidance on assessment activities or processes (e.g. practice questions or advice on how to answer assessment questions), included in the resource nor does it prescribe any particular approach to the teaching or delivery of a related course.

While the publishers have made every attempt to ensure that advice on the qualification and its assessment is accurate, the official specification and associated assessment guidance materials are the only authoritative source of information and should always be referred to for definitive guidance. Pearson examiners have not contributed to any sections in this resource relevant to examination papers for which they have responsibility. Examiners will not use endorsed resources as a source of material for any assessment set by Pearson. Endorsement of a resource does not mean that the resource is required to achieve this Pearson qualification, nor does it mean that it is the only suitable material available to support the qualification, and any resource lists produced by the awarding body shall include this and other appropriate resources.

The publisher would like to thank the following for permission to reproduce copyright material.

Acknowledgements

The Holy Bible, New International Version ®, NIV ®. Copyright Copyright © 1973, 1978, 1984, 2011 by Biblica, Inc. ® Used by permission. All rights reserved worldwide; *The Catechism of the Catholic Church* by Geoffrey Chapman, (Continuum, 2002); *The Holy Qur'an* by Tom Griffith, trans. Abdullah Yusuf Ali, (Wordsworth Editions, 2000).

Hodder Education, an Hachette UK company, Carmelite House, 50 Victoria Embankment, London EC4Y 0DZ

Orders: please contact Bookpoint Ltd, 130 Park Drive, Milton Park, Abingdon, Oxon OX14 4SE. Tel: 01235 827720. Fax: 01235 400454. Lines are open 9.00 a.m.–5.00 p.m., Monday to Saturday, with a 24-hour message answering service. You can also order through our website: www.hoddereducation.co.uk

ISBN 9781510404786

First published in 2017

Impression number 5 4

Year 2021 2020 2019

Typeset in India by Integra Software Serv. Ltd

Printed in India

Hachette UK's policy is to use papers that are natural, renewable and recyclable products and made from wood grown in sustainable forests. The logging and manufacturing processes are expected to conform to the environmental regulations of the country of origin.

Get the most from this book

Everyone has to decide his or her own revision strategy, but it is essential to review your work, learn it and test your understanding. These Revisions Notes will help you to do that in a planned way, topic by topic. Use this book as the cornerstone of your revision and don't hesitate to write in it – personalise your notes and check your progress by ticking off each section as you revise.

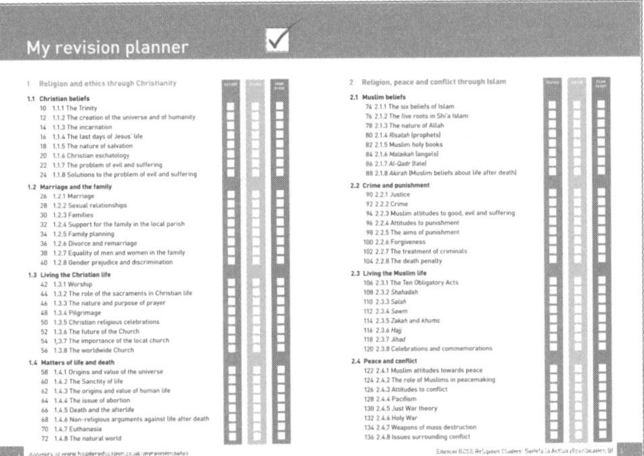

My revision planner

1 Religion and ethics through Christianity

1.1 Christian beliefs
10 1.1.1 The Trinity
12 1.1.2 The creation of the universe and of humanity
14 1.1.3 The incarnation
16 1.1.4 The last days of Jesus' life
18 1.1.5 The nature of salvation
20 1.1.6 Christian eschatology
22 1.1.7 The problem of evil and suffering
24 1.1.8 Solutions to the problem of evil and suffering

1.2 Marriage and the family
26 1.2.1 Marriage
28 1.2.2 Sexual relationships
30 1.2.3 Families
32 1.2.4 Support for the family in the local parish
34 1.2.5 Family planning
36 1.2.6 Divorce and remarriage
38 1.2.7 Equality of men and women in the family
40 1.2.8 Gender prejudice and discrimination

1.3 Living the Christian life
42 1.3.1 Worship
44 1.3.2 The role of the sacraments in Christian life
46 1.3.3 The nature and purpose of prayer
48 1.3.4 Pilgrimage
50 1.3.5 Christian religious celebrations
52 1.3.6 The future of the Church
54 1.3.7 The importance of the local church
56 1.3.8 The worldwide Church

1.4 Matters of life and death
58 1.4.1 Origins and value of the universe
60 1.4.2 The Sanctity of life
62 1.4.3 The origins and value of human life
64 1.4.4 The issue of abortion
66 1.4.5 Death and the afterlife
68 1.4.6 Non-religious arguments against life after death
70 1.4.7 Euthanasia
72 1.4.8 The natural world

2 Religion, peace and conflict through Islam

2.1 Muslim beliefs
74 2.1.1 The six beliefs of Islam
76 2.1.2 The five roots in Shi'a Islam
78 2.1.3 The nature of Allah
80 2.1.4 *Risalah* (prophets)
82 2.1.5 Muslim holy books
84 2.1.6 *Malaikah* (angels)
86 2.1.7 *Al-Qadr* (fate)
88 2.1.8 *Akirah* (Muslim beliefs about life after death)

2.2 Crime and punishment
90 2.2.1 Justice
92 2.2.2 Crime
94 2.2.3 Muslim attitudes to good, evil and suffering
96 2.2.4 Attitudes to punishment
98 2.2.5 The aims of punishment
100 2.2.6 Forgiveness
102 2.2.7 The treatment of criminals
104 2.2.8 The death penalty

2.3 Living the Muslim life
106 2.3.1 The Ten Obligatory Acts
108 2.3.2 *Shahadah*
110 2.3.3 *Salah*
112 2.3.4 *Sawm*
114 2.3.5 *Zakah* and *khums*
116 2.3.6 *Hajj*
118 2.3.7 *Jihad*
120 2.3.8 Celebrations and commemorations

2.4 Peace and conflict
122 2.4.1 Muslim attitudes towards peace
124 2.4.2 The role of Muslims in peacemaking
126 2.4.3 Attitudes to conflict
128 2.4.4 Pacifism
130 2.4.5 Just War theory
132 2.4.6 Holy War
134 2.4.7 Weapons of mass destruction
136 2.4.8 Issues surrounding conflict

Tick to track your progress

Use the revision planner on pages 4 and 5 to plan your revision, topic by topic. Tick each box when you have:

- revised and understood a topic
- tested yourself
- practised the exam questions and checked your answers online.

You can also keep track of your revision by ticking off each topic heading in the book. You may find it helpful to add your own notes as you work through each topic.

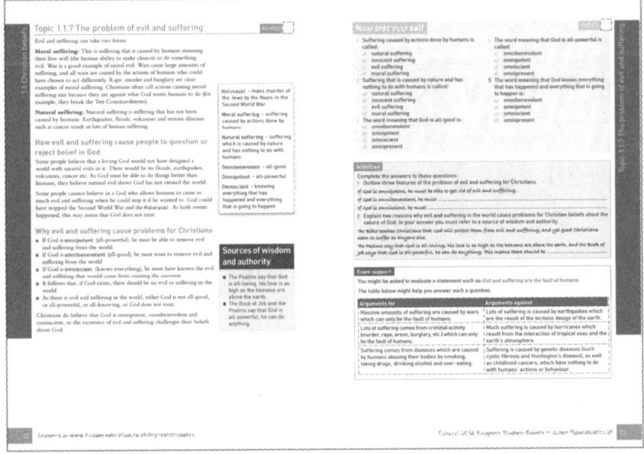

Topic 1.1.7 The problem of evil and suffering

Features to help you succeed

Now test yourself

These short, knowledge-based questions provide the first steps in testing your learning. Answers are provided online.

Definitions and key words

Clear, concise definitions of essential key terms are provided where they first appear.

Key words from the specification are highlighted in bold throughout the book.

Revision activities

These activities will help you to understand each topic in an interactive way. Answers are provided online.

Exam support

Exam support boxes are provided for each topic. Read them to help breakdown exam questions and form useful planning tools for the exam.

Online

Go online to check your answers to the Now Test Yourself and activity questions.

My revision planner

1 Religion and ethics through Christianity

REVISED | TESTED | EXAM READY

2 Religion, peace and conflict through Islam

REVISED | TESTED | EXAM READY

2.1 Muslim beliefs

2.2 Crime and punishment

2.3 Living the Muslim life

2.4 Peace and conflict

How to use this book

This book provides a revision guide for the Edexcel GCSE Religious Studies Specification B: Area of Study 1 Religion and Ethics through Christianity and Area of Study 2 Religion, Peace and Conflict through Islam.

Each chapter of the book is one of the eight sections of the GCSE specification, and each chapter is divided into the eight topics of the specification. Each topic has the main points you need to know. In the margin is a box with the specialist terms you will find useful. Under this is another box with some sources of authority which you will need to learn for the c) questions.

On the opposite page are three sections aimed at improving your exam performance (answers are found online).

- The Now Test Yourself is set of multiple-choice questions. You won't have multiple-choice questions in the exam, but these will help you check your knowledge.
- Each activity is in two parts. Part 1 is a typical a) question where the beginning of an answer has been provided for you to complete. Part 2 is a typical c) question which you need to complete. These activities provide you with guidance to give you an idea of what is expected in the exam.
- Exam support sets out some arguments for and against the issues raised by the topic to make it easier for you to answer the evaluation questions. But remember that in the exam, you will need to evaluate the arguments and write a conclusion about the issue to get more than half of the available marks.

How the assessment works

Each Area of Study is assessed by a **1 hour 45 minutes** examination which has four questions, one on each section of the specification.

All the questions follow the same format i.e. they are divided into four sub-questions.

Part a) questions

These assess knowledge and might ask you to outline facts, for example, 'Outline three Christian beliefs about marriage.'

Each outline will gain you a mark and you should spend no more than 4 minutes answering these questions.

Example:

Christians believe that marriage is the only acceptable way for Christians to have sexual relationships (one correct belief = 1 mark). They believe that marriage is for life (two correct beliefs = 2 marks) and that marriage should be between one man and one woman (three correct beliefs = 3 marks).

Part b) questions

These assess understanding and will usually ask you to explain, for example, 'Explain two reasons why the Trinity is important to Christians.'

There will be one mark for each reason and a second mark for developing it, and you should spend no more than 4 minutes answering these questions.

Example:

Christians feel that the Trinity is important because it helps them understand how the one God works in the world (1 mark) through the three persons of: the Father who creates, the Son who saves from sin, the Spirit who empowers (development so 2 marks). They also believe it helps them understand God's unity (3 marks). The three persons have only one substance – God, the three in one (development so 4 marks).

Part c) questions

These also ask you to explain, but they also require you to refer to a source of wisdom and authority, for example, 'Explain two reasons why Christian teachings about sexual relationships are important today. In your answer you must refer to a source of wisdom and authority.'

There will be one mark for each reason and a second mark for developing it, plus an extra mark for referring to a source of wisdom and authority, and you should spend no more than 6 minutes answering these questions.

Example:

Christian teachings are important because many people today think sex before marriage and cohabitation are all right, but many Christian Churches says they are wrong (1 mark for a reason) because of the teachings on sexual ethics in the Bible such as St Paul condemning sexual immorality in 1 Corinthians (2 marks for development). Also the Catechism of the Catholic Church says that 'the sexual act must always take place exclusively within marriage' (+1 mark for reference to a source of wisdom and authority). The teachings are also important because many people nowadays think homosexuality is acceptable, but Catholic and Evangelical Protestant Christians believe that although homosexual feelings are acceptable, homosexual acts are wrong because they are condemned in the Bible (4 marks). St Paul says in his letter to the Romans that homosexual acts are 'shameful lusts' (5 marks).

Part d) questions

These questions require you to make a reasoned evaluation of a controversial statement by looking at arguments for and against to decide whether the statement is true. To answer these questions, you should:

- Read the bullet points under the statement carefully to see whether you need to refer to two different points of view among Christians (you could refer to Protestants and Catholics) or two different points of view among Muslims (you could refer to liberal and traditional). If the question asks you to refer to non-religious points of view, you should use a Christian or Muslim point of view and non-religious points of view.
- When you have decided how the question wants you to evaluate the statement, you need to analyse the validity of the arguments used by those who would agree with the statement (i.e. explain whether and why each reason is convincing).
- Next analyse the validity of the arguments used by people who disagree (i.e. explaining whether and why each reason is convincing).
- Most importantly you must then come to a conclusion that your analysis has led you to by making a reasoned judgement about the statement on the basis of the most convincing set of arguments.
- It is possible that the arguments are evenly balanced because there are good points on each side, in which case you should conclude with something like the following. 'The arguments are evenly balanced and the truth of the statement will depend on the beliefs of the person looking at it. Most Catholic Christians would think the statement is correct because they believe in the Magisterium of the Church and so they think that … However, many Protestant Christians would think the statement is incorrect because they believe in the primacy of the Bible and so they think that … '
- **Never use bullet points in** d) question answers.

Strong arguments are likely to be based on sources of authority:

- Based on what a holy book (Bible, Qur'an, Hadith) says
- Based on what the official teachings say (Creeds, Catechism, Six Beliefs, Ten Acts, Shari'ah)
- Based on what religious leaders say (Papal Encyclicals, decisions of Church Synods, conferences of bishops etc, fatwas of imams, decisions by councils of Muslim lawyers, decisions by Shi'a Ayatolloahs)
- Based on scientific evidence
- Based on the laws of a country
- Based on experience

Weak arguments are likely to be:

- Based on personal opinion
- Based on someone's interpretation of a religious text
- Based on what everybody thinks/popular ideas
- Based on a minority view in a religion
- Ignorant of religious teachings

You should spend no more than 12 minutes answering these questions.

Example of a high-level answer

(d) "The biblical account of creation is a metaphor."

Evaluate this statement considering arguments for and against. In your response you should:

- refer to Christian teachings
- reach a justified conclusion. (15)

Most Liberal Christians would argue that this statement is correct because they believe the Bible is a book of words about God, but not God's words, and so what the Bible says about creation is going to be a metaphor rather than a factual account as the authors did not witness the creation. Such Christians believe that scientific study of the Bible shows that chapters 1–2 and chapter 3 of Genesis have different authors and contradict each other (Genesis 3 says man was made before vegetation and animals) and so they must be metaphorical rather than factual. This is a strong argument because it is based on scientific analysis of the Bible. They also believe it must be a metaphor because the Bible account contradicts science which provides evidence for creation taking billions of years not six days and coming through evolution not God's direct intervention, another strong argument based on science.

However, Conservative and Literalist Christians criticise this argument as they believe the biblical account of creation must be factually correct because they believe the Bible is the word of God, as St Paul said in 2 Timothy, 'All scripture is inspired by God and profitable for teaching.' This is a strong Christian argument as it is based on the Bible, which is the ultimate source of authority for Christians. Also, many Catholic Christians would think the statement is incorrect because the Catechism says that the books of the Bible teach the truth and so the creation account cannot be a metaphor. This is another strong Christian argument because the Catechism is the official teaching of the Church, the Magisterium, which all Catholics should believe.

The truth of this statement seems to depend on whether science is given more weight than the Bible. Those who think the Bible is the exact words of God are always going to think the statement is incorrect. However, Pope Francis has recently declared his support for the scientific view of creation being fact and therefore for Genesis being a metaphor, and the Pope is a major source of authority for Catholics. It can also be argued that Genesis can be both a metaphor and the word of God as there is no reason why God shouldn't use metaphors, and so it would seem the statement is most likely correct.

This answer is a high-level answer because:

- It addresses all the elements of the question (different Christian views of the statement are analysed and evaluated).
- There is a logical chain of reasoning throughout as the answer links the arguments for and against with each argument underpinned by clear understanding of religion and belief: 'they believe the biblical account of creation must be factually correct because they believe the Bible is the word of God, as St Paul said in 2 Timothy, "All Scripture is inspired by God and profitable for teaching." This is a strong Christian argument as it is based on the Bible, the ultimate source of authority.'
- There is a coherence to the response, in the sense that all of the arguments are drawn together well, and the arguments are appraised throughout the answer with preliminary judgements: 'The Catechism says that the books of the Bible teach the truth and so the creation account cannot be a metaphor. A strong argument because the Catechism is the official teaching of the Church, the Magisterium, which all Catholics should believe.'
- There is a fully justified conclusion where the candidate brings together all the points that they have been making throughout: 'However, Pope Francis has recently declared his support for the scientific view of creation being fact and therefore for Genesis being a metaphor, and the Pope is a major source of authority for Catholics. It can also be argued that Genesis can be both a metaphor and the word of God.... and so it would seem the statement is most likely correct.'

The part d) questions for Sections 1 and 3 also have 3 marks for spelling punctuation and grammar.

- 1 mark is awarded for candidates who spell and punctuate with reasonable accuracy, use rules of grammar to control meaning and use a limited range of specialist terms.
- 2 marks are awarded for candidates who spell and punctuate with considerable accuracy, use rules of grammar with general control of meaning overall and use a good range of specialist terms.
- 3 marks are awarded for candidates who spell and punctuate with consistent accuracy, use rules of grammar with effective control of meaning and use a wide range of specialist terms.

The sample answer above would be awarded 3 marks because spelling, punctuation and grammar is correct, meaning is clear and a wide range of specialist terms (Liberal, Conservative, Literalist, Genesis, St Paul, 2 Timothy, Catechism, Pope Francis, Magisterium) are used appropriately.

Sources of wisdom and authority do not need exact quotes or references to chapter and verse. The question c) answers in the activities show you what is needed to gain a mark.

- Sources of wisdom and authority for Christianity might include the Bible, the Creeds, the Catholic Catechism, Papal Encyclicals, other statements by the Pope, pastoral advice from bishops.
- Sources of wisdom and authority for Islam might include Qur'an, Hadith, Sunna, Six Beliefs, Ten Acts, fatwas, decisions by Muslim lawyers or, for Shi'as, Ayatollahs.

The activities after each topic give you a chance to practise the a) and c) questions with some help. The exam support after each topic gives you ideas for arguments for and against in the d) questions, but you must write your own evaluation and conclusion.

1.1 Christian beliefs

Topic 1.1.1 The Trinity

REVISED

The nature of the Trinity and the oneness of God

Believing in the oneness of God is the basis of Christianity – it is a **monotheistic** religion. Christians believe that God reveals himself to the world in three persons (the Holy Trinity). The **Nicene Creed** explains that there is one Being – God – experienced as three persons – Father, Son and Holy Spirit – who are all equal and all eternal.

Christians feel that belief in the individual persons of the Trinity helps them understand the different ways that God has shown his presence in the world:

- God the Father helps Christians understand his power and creativity and his care for the world and its peoples.
- God the Son (Jesus) helps Christians understand the love of God, the sacrifice of God leading to **salvation** from **sin** and the promise of eternal life.
- God the Holy Spirit helps Christians to understand the presence of God in the world. Christians believe that the Holy Spirit is the means by which God communicates with humans.

How the Trinity is shown in belief and worship

Belief in the Trinity is expressed in all forms of Christian worship:

- Christians express their belief in the Trinity when they repeat the Nicene Creed in every service of **Holy Communion** (the **Eucharist** or Mass).
- Many Christians express their belief in the Trinity by crossing themselves when they enter a church or when the name of the Trinity is mentioned.
- Priests/ministers/pastors usually begin their sermons with the words, 'In the name of the Father, and of the Son and of the Holy Spirit', and bless the congregation in the name of the Trinity at the end of services.
- Baptisms and marriages are performed in the name of the Trinity.

Many Christians find the Trinity a difficult concept, but believe it because they have experienced God as the Father, and as the Son and as the Holy Spirit. However, some Christian groups, such as Mormons and Jehovah's Witnesses, do not accept the belief in the Trinity.

Sources of wisdom and authority

Always remember that the Gospels, and any Bible book or teachings are sources of wisdom and authority for Christians.

- God the Trinity is shown in Matthew's account of the baptism of Jesus where the Father declares Jesus to be the Son, and the Spirit descends as a dove.
- The **Catechism** says that the Trinity is a holy mystery central to the Christian faith

Catechism – the official teaching of the Catholic Church

Eucharist – a sacrament commemorating the Last Supper of Jesus

Holy Communion – the Christian service of thanksgiving using bread and wine (also called Eucharist or Mass)

Monotheism – belief in one God

Nicene Creed – statement of Christian belief accepted by most Christians

Salvation – the act of delivering from sin or saving from evil

Sin – an act that is against God's will

Now test yourself

TESTED

1 What is the Nicene Creed?
   a) The agreed statement of Christian belief
   b) A statement about Christian beliefs
   c) The statement of Christian belief agreed by Catholic and Orthodox Christians
   d) A statement about the Trinity

2 What is monotheism?
   a) Belief in God
   b) Belief in the Christian God
   c) Belief in one God
   d) Belief in many gods

3 An act against God's will is known as:
   a) salvation
   b) sin
   c) Catechism
   d) Eucharist

4 What is the official teaching of the Catholic Church known as?
   a) Salvation
   b) Sin
   c) Catechism
   d) Eucharist

Activities

Complete the answers to these questions:

1 Outline three ways in which belief in the Trinity is shown in Christian worship.

Christians show their belief in the Trinity when they repeat the Nicene Creed in every service of Holy Communion. Another way is ....

A third way is ....

2 Explain two reasons why Christians believe in the Trinity. In your answer you must refer to a source of wisdom and authority.

Christians believe in the Trinity because it is taught in the Gospels. In Matthew's account of the baptism of Jesus, Jesus the Son goes under the water and, as he comes up, God the Holy Spirit descends on him like a dove and then God the Father says this is his Son.

Another reason is that ....

Exam support

You might be asked to evaluate a statement such as:

You can't be a Christian if you don't believe in the Trinity.

The table below might help you answer such a question.

Arguments for	Arguments against
The Nicene Creed contains a statement of belief in the Trinity.	Jesus said the most important things were to love God and love your neighbour.
The Catechism of the Catholic Church says the Trinity is central to Christian belief and life.	Christians such as Mormons and Jehovah's Witnesses do not believe in the Trinity.
Churches can only be members of the World Council of Churches if they believe in the Trinity.	Jesus said, 'by their fruits shall you know them', meaning that what you do is more important than what you believe.

Topic 1.1.2 The creation of the universe and of humanity

REVISED

There are two different biblical accounts of creation in Genesis:

- Genesis chapter 1 says that God created the universe in six days, starting with the earth and heaven on day 1 and culminating with the creation of humans (male and female) on day 6. Everything God made was good and on day 7 he rested, making that day holy.
- Genesis chapters 2–3 say that God created man (Adam) immediately after creating the heavens and the earth and placed him in the Garden of Eden. He saw Adam was lonely and so created birds and animals for him. When this did not work God created woman (Eve) from Adam's rib and they lived in the garden until they disobeyed God and were sent out into the world.

Christians understand these stories in different ways:

1. **Literalist Christians** believe the Bible is the literal word of God and that both Genesis 1 and 2 are scientific truth. Genesis 1 gives the overall picture of creation and Genesis 2 and 3 give details of day 6 when God created humans and animals. Literalist Christians do not accept the scientific idea of the **Big Bang** and **evolution**.
2. **Conservative Christians** believe the Bible is the word of God, but not his actual words, and that Genesis 2 and 3 are poetic explanations of Genesis 1. They don't believe that either Genesis 1 or 2 are absolute scientific fact (though they think Genesis 1 is fairly factual if a day is defined as billions of years rather than 24 hours). They accept the Big Bang and evolution.
3. **Liberal Christians** believe the Bible is a book of words about God, but not God's words, and that Genesis 1 and Genesis 2–3 had different authors and are metaphors about creation rather than factual. They believe the importance of biblical creation is that it shows the universe was created by God and that that creation was good.

John's Gospel records that creation came through the word of God (who John identifies as Jesus). Most Christians believe that when this teaching is combined with the references to the Spirit of God in Genesis 1–3, it means that the Bible teaches that creation came through the Trinity.

The beliefs about creation are important for Christians today because they show that:

- the world is good
- God created humans in his image, meaning they have **self-knowledge** and **free will** so they can choose between good and evil
- God gave people **human dignity** and responsibility for God's creation, so they have **stewardship** of the earth, meaning God expects humans to pass on a better earth than they entered
- how well people perform as stewards will determine how they are judged by God after death.

Big Bang – the explosion which scientists believe began the universe

Conservative Christians – those who believe the Bible is the word of God, but not his actual words; it may not have the literal truth but all its teachings should be followed

Evolution – the theory that life on earth developed from simple forms through the process of natural selection

Free will – the idea that human beings are free to make their own choices

Human dignity – the belief that humans are persons, not things, and that they have self-knowledge and free will

Liberal Christians – those who believe the Bible is a book of words about God, and so it needs re-interpreting in light of the modern world

Literalist Christians – those who believe the Bible is the actual word of God and the literal truth

Self-knowledge – knowing who you are and why you are here

Stewardship – looking after something so it can be passed on to the next generation

Sources of wisdom and authority

- Genesis 1 says that God saw all that he had made and it was good.
- The Catechism of the Catholic Church says that being made in the image of God means that humans have dignity, self-knowledge and free will.
- John's Gospel says that the Word was at the beginning and everything was made through the Word.

Now test yourself

TESTED

1 Knowing who you are and why you are here is:
   a) human dignity
   b) free will
   c) self-knowledge
   d) stewardship
2 Christians who believe the Bible is God's words are called:
   a) liberals
   b) conservatives
   c) literalists
   d) evangelicals
3 Being able to choose between good and evil requires:
   a) human dignity
   b) free will
   c) self-knowledge
   d) stewardship
4 Christians who believe the Bible needs re-interpreting in light of the modern world are:
   a) liberals
   b) conservatives
   c) literalists
   d) evangelicals

Activities

Complete the answers to these questions:

1 Outline three features of the creation described in Genesis 1.

One feature is that God created everything in six days. Another feature is that God created male and female together. A third feature is that when God saw what he had made ....

2 Explain two different interpretations of the accounts of creation in Genesis. In your answer you must refer to a source of wisdom and authority.

Christians who believe the Bible is the literal word of God (literalists) believe that both Genesis 1 and 2 are scientific truth. Genesis 1 gives the overall picture and Genesis 2–3 give details of day six. They believe that the scientific ideas of Big Bang and evolution are wrong.

Liberal Christians believe ....

Exam support

You might be asked to evaluate a statement such as:

It is hard to believe the biblical accounts of creation.

The table below might help you answer such a question.

Arguments for	Arguments against
Science shows that the creation of the universe took billions of years, not six days.	If the Bible is the word of God, then it must be true and so is easy to believe.
Science shows that humans evolved from other species of mammals, not that they were suddenly created by God.	It is easier to believe that God created the universe than that this huge complex system was just an accident.
Science has evidence such as the Red-shift effect and the fossil record.	It is easy to explain the different accounts in Genesis if chapters 2–3 are poetic explanations of chapter 1.
There are two Bible accounts which seem to contradict each other.	Genesis is factual when a day is defined as billions of years rather than 24 hours.

Topic 1.1.3 The incarnation

REVISED

Jesus, the incarnate Son of God

Christians believe that God became a human being in Jesus Christ. They believe that Jesus did not have a normal conception but that he did have a normal birth. They believe his mother, Mary, was a virgin who conceived Jesus by the Holy Spirit. This is known as the **virgin birth** and is an important belief because if Jesus was conceived by sex he would be a normal human, not God. Our knowledge of Jesus and his incarnation comes from the **Gospels** of Matthew, Luke and John.

The biblical basis of the incarnation

- Matthew's Gospel says Mary's husband-to-be, Joseph, was told about the conception by an angel, he married Mary, who was a virgin, and Jesus was born in Bethlehem. The family was visited by wise men who worshipped Jesus. King Herod saw Jesus as a threat to his power and tried to kill the baby, but Joseph escaped with his family to Egypt and they only returned to Nazareth after Herod had died.
- Luke's Gospel says Mary was visited by an angel and that she and Joseph travelled from Nazareth to Bethlehem because of a Roman census. Jesus was born in Bethlehem and was visited by shepherds who had been told of Jesus' birth by angels. The family then returned to Nazareth via Jerusalem.
- John's Gospel records the **incarnation** in **theological** language, rather than as a story, recording that Jesus was the Word who was with God at the beginning and became flesh at the incarnation.

The significance of the incarnation

Christians believe the incarnation is significant or important because:

- it shows God's love in sending his Son to show humans what God is like and to teach them how to live
- it is the basis of the Christian faith; without the incarnation of Jesus Christ there would be no Christianity
- in Jesus, the incarnate Son of God, humans can see what God is like
- through the incarnation, God began the process of salvation from sin, making it possible for humans to have a full relationship with God and to go to heaven after death.

Sources of wisdom and authority

- John's Gospel says that Jesus was the Word made flesh.
- The Virgin Mary's conception, the birth of Jesus in Bethlehem and his recognition as the Son of God by shepherds and wise men is recorded in the Gospels of Matthew and Luke.

Gospels – the books of the Bible (Matthew, Mark, Luke and John), which are the only record of Jesus' life

Incarnation – the belief that God took human form in Jesus

Theological – relating to the academic study of God and religious ideas

Virgin birth – the belief that Jesus was not conceived through sex

Now test yourself

TESTED

1 The academic study of God and religious ideas is known as:
   a) incarnation
   b) salvation
   c) theology
   d) virgin birth
2 Deliverance from sin and its consequences is known as:
   a) incarnation
   b) salvation
   c) theology
   d) virgin birth
3 The belief that Jesus was not conceived through sex is central to the idea of:
   a) incarnation
   b) salvation
   c) theology
   d) virgin birth
4 The belief that God took human form in Jesus is known as:
   a) incarnation
   b) salvation
   c) theology
   d) virgin birth

Activities

Complete the answers to these questions:

1 Outline three features of the birth story as described in Matthew's Gospel.

One feature in Matthew's Gospel says Mary's husband-to-be, Joseph, was told about the conception by an angel. Another feature is ....

A third feature is that ....

2 Explain two reasons why Christians believe Jesus was God incarnate. In your answer you must refer to a source of wisdom and authority.

Christians believe in the incarnation because without the belief that God became human in Jesus, there would be no Christianity. John's Gospel says that Jesus was the word made flesh.

Another reason Christians believe Jesus was God incarnate is ....

Exam support

You might be asked to evaluate a statement such as:

Jesus was God incarnate.

The table below might help you answer such a question.

Arguments for	Arguments against
Jesus had a virgin birth and only God could be born of a virgin.	The only evidence for the incarnation is the Bible and there is no reason for believing the Bible is the truth.
Jesus performed miracles, like stilling a storm, which only God could do.	The accounts in Matthew and Luke contradict each other – did the family return to Nazareth or go to Egypt?
Jesus rose from the dead which only God could do.	A human being requires male and female genes, so if Jesus was a human being, where did his male genes come from?
It is the teaching of all the Christian Churches and Creeds.	God is supposed to be an infinite being but Jesus was a finite being, which means Jesus could not have been God.

Topic 1.1.4 The last days of Jesus' life

REVISED

The last days of Jesus are the basis of the Christian faith. They cover all that happened from the Last Supper to the **ascension**. You need to know the events as they are recorded in Luke's Gospel (chapters 22–24).

The Last Supper: The night before he was crucified, Jesus shared a meal with his **disciples** in Jerusalem when he **prophesied** that one of his disciples would betray him. At the end of the meal he shared bread and wine with the disciples, saying the bread was his body and the wine his blood, so establishing the Eucharist. During a discussion about greatness, Jesus said the greatest are those who serve and that Peter would deny knowing Jesus three times before morning.

The betrayal and arrest: After supper, Jesus left the disciples while he went to pray, asking God to 'take this cup from me, yet not my will but yours be done'. When he went back, the disciples were asleep. As they awoke, Judas Iscariot, one of the disciples, arrived with the chief priests to arrest Jesus. The disciples wanted to fight, but Jesus wouldn't let them.

The trial: Peter followed Jesus to the house of the Chief Priest but denied he knew Jesus when he was challenged. Jesus was then tried by the **Sanhedrin** and found guilty of **blasphemy** for claiming to be 'the Christ, the Son of God'. He was then taken for trial by the Roman governor **Pontius Pilate**, who could not find him guilty of anything and offered to release Jesus or Barabbas (a Jewish freedom fighter). The crowd chose Barabbas and Jesus was condemned to death by **crucifixion**.

The crucifixion: The four Gospels agree that Jesus was crucified on a Friday (Good Friday), Simon of Cyrene carried the cross for Jesus, a robber was crucified on either side of Jesus and Jesus was mocked by the bystanders. Jesus forgave his killers and died with the words, 'Father into your hands I commit my spirit.'

The resurrection: Joseph of Arimathea (a member of the Sanhedrin) got permission to bury Jesus' body in his tomb. On Sunday morning (now known as Easter Day) Jesus' women followers came to anoint the body but they found the tomb empty. They told the disciples who confirmed it. Jesus then appeared to two disciples at a village near Jerusalem called Emmaus.

The ascension: Jesus continued to appear for 40 days then he told his remaining disciples to wait in Jerusalem for the gift of the Holy Spirit and then Jesus was taken up from them into a cloud.

Ascension – the return of Christ to heaven

Blasphemy – speaking disrespectfully about God or sacred things

Crucifixion – the Roman method of execution by hanging on a cross

Disciples – the twelve men chosen by Jesus to be his followers

Pontius Pilate – the Roman governor of Judea

Prophesied – predicted events in the future

Resurrection – rising from the dead

Sanhedrin – the supreme religious authority in Israel at the time of Jesus

Differences in the records of the other Gospels

- John does not mention bread and wine at the Last Supper but does record Jesus washing his disciples' feet.
- John says Joseph of Arimathea anointed the body before burial.
- Matthew says Pilate put guards on the tomb but they were frightened away when an earthquake rolled the stone from the tomb's entrance.
- Matthew, Mark and John record resurrection appearances in Galilee.

Importance of these events

- The Last Supper is the basis of the Eucharist, the most important form of Christian worship.
- Christians believe the crucifixion brought forgiveness from sin.
- The resurrection assures Christians that there is life after death.
- The ascension assures Christians that Jesus is no longer restricted by a body and can be with them anywhere.

Sources of wisdom and authority

- Luke's Gospel says that, at the Last Supper, Jesus said the bread was his body and the wine was his blood.
- Luke's Gospel says Jesus asked God to forgive those crucifying him.

Now test yourself

TESTED

1 The ascension was when:
   a) Jesus Christ was raised from the dead
   b) Jesus Christ returned to heaven
   c) Jesus Christ established the Eucharist
   d) Jesus Christ saved the world from sin
2 Blasphemy means:
   a) swearing
   b) denying God's existence
   c) speaking disrespectfully about God
   d) being an atheist
3 Which of these did Jesus *not* do at the Last Supper?
   a) Washed his disciples' feet
   b) Prophesied his ascension
   c) Gave the disciples bread and wine
   d) Prophesied that a disciple would betray him
4 Which of these events do Christians believe did *not* happen on Easter Day?
   a) Jesus' women followers found an empty tomb
   b) Jesus appeared to the disciples
   c) Jesus told his disciples to wait in Jerusalem for the Holy Spirit
   d) Jesus appeared in Emmaus

Activities

Complete the answers to these questions:

1 Outline three features of the account of the trials of Jesus according to Luke's Gospel.

One feature of the trial before the Sanhedrin is that they found Jesus guilty of blasphemy. Another feature is that the Sanhedrin sent Jesus to be tried by Pontius Pilate. Another feature is that at this trial ....

2 Explain two reasons why the events of his last days show the importance of Jesus. In your answer you must refer to a source of wisdom and authority.

The Last Supper is the basis of the Eucharist, the most important form of Christian worship, when the priest/minister blesses bread and wine using the words of Jesus. The congregation then use the words of Jesus, 'this is my body' when they share the bread and 'this is my blood' when they share the wine.

The ascension also shows the importance of Jesus because ....

Exam support

You might be asked to evaluate a statement such as:

The resurrection was the most important event in the life of Jesus.

The table below might help you answer such a question.

Arguments for	Arguments against
The resurrection proves that Jesus was the Son of God.	The crucifixion is equally important because it brought the forgiveness of sins without which Christians cannot get to heaven.
The resurrection is the basis of Christian belief as St Paul said, 'If Christ has not been raised, our preaching is useless and so is your faith' (1 Corinthians).	The Sermon on the Mount is also important because it records Jesus teaching Christians how to live their lives.
The resurrection of Jesus is the basis of the Christian belief in life after death and the promise that death is not the end.	The incarnation is important because without God becoming flesh in Jesus there could have been no resurrection.
The resurrection guarantees eternal life to Christians.	The Last Supper is just as important as without it there would be no Eucharist and no sharing of Christ's body and blood.

Topic 1.1.5 The nature of salvation

REVISED

The nature of salvation

Many Christians believe that the perfect relationship between God and humans was broken by the sin of Adam and Eve, which resulted in everyone being born with **original sin**, as well as having their own sins. Christians believe that salvation is needed to restore the relationship with God and have eternal life in heaven.

The role of Jesus in salvation

At the time of Jesus, Jewish people believed that salvation came through obeying the **Law** given to Moses. However, Christians believe that Jesus came to earth to bring salvation to the world. They believe that when Jesus died on the cross, his death paid the price for human sins and gave people the chance of salvation. Christians often call this **atonement** (which means **reconciliation**) – Jesus' death atones for human sins and heals the broken relationship between humans and God.

Catholic, Orthodox and some Anglican Christians believe they receive Jesus' salvation by receiving the sacraments, especially baptism, confirmation, reconciliation/confession and the Eucharist and by leading a Christian life. Evangelical Protestants believe salvation comes through a personal acceptance of Jesus as Lord and Saviour. Liberal Protestants believe salvation comes through living a Christian life. All Christians believe that salvation brings God's **grace** (the strength to be good and holy).

Why salvation is important to Christians

Christians believe salvation is important because:

- without salvation there can be no real relationship with God
- without salvation a person's sins will prevent them entering heaven
- salvation from sin was the whole purpose of Jesus coming to earth and founding Christianity.

Divergent Christian understandings of atonement

Christians use the word 'atonement' to describe how the death and resurrection of Jesus pardoned sin, especially original sin, and allowed God to be reconciled with his creation. However, different Christians understand atonement in different ways:

- The Catholic Church teaches that Jesus' death was an act of self-sacrifice (Christ's Passion) which made 'satisfaction' for human sins making salvation possible for all through taking the **sacraments** of the Church.
- Evangelical Protestants believe that God's justice required a price to be paid for human sin (punishment) and that rather than punish humans, God took the punishment on himself through the death of Christ, who acted as a substitute for the whole of humanity (penal substitution theory). Salvation comes through **faith** in the atoning death of Christ.
- Liberal Protestants believe that Jesus brought about atonement through his moral example and love for humanity (as seen in his undeserved death), which inspires Christians to live a good life and be reconciled with God.

Atonement – reconciliation between God and humans

Faith – firm belief without logical proof

Grace – God's gift which gives the strength to be good and holy

Law – the 613 commands given to Moses by God

Original sin – the sin of Adam and Eve disobeying God, which some Christians believe is passed on to all humans at birth

Reconciliation – bringing together people who were opposed to each other

Sacrament – an outward ceremony through which God's grace is given

Sources of wisdom and authority

- John's Gospel says that God so loved the world that he sent his only Son to save the world.
- St Paul says in his letters that salvation can only be found in Jesus.

Now test yourself

TESTED

1 Reconciliation is:
   a) firm belief without logical proof
   b) bringing together people who were opposed to each other
   c) the act of delivering from sin or saving from evil
   d) an act that is against God's will
2 Atonement is:
   a) reconciliation between God and humans
   b) bringing together people who were opposed to each other
   c) the act of delivering from sin or saving from evil
   d) an act that is against God's will
3 Faith is:
   a) reconciliation between God and humans.
   b) firm belief without logical proof
   c) bringing together people who were opposed to each other
   d) the act of delivering from sin or saving from evil
4 Sin is:
   a) reconciliation between God and humans
   b) firm belief without logical proof
   c) bringing together people who were opposed to each other
   d) an act that is against God's will

Activities

Complete the answers to these questions:

1 Outline three different understandings of atonement.

The Catholic Church teaches that Jesus' death was an act of self-sacrifice which made satisfaction for human sins and made salvation possible. Evangelical Protestants believe that God's justice required a price to be paid for sin and God took the punishment on himself through the death of Christ.

Liberal Protestants believe ....

2 Explain two reasons why Christians believe salvation is important. In your answer you must refer to a source of wisdom and authority.

For Catholics and Evangelical Protestants salvation is important because without salvation from sin, people cannot have eternal life or enter heaven. St Paul said in his letters that salvation can only be found in Jesus.

Salvation is important for Liberal Christians because ....

Exam support

You might be asked to evaluate a statement such as:

Only those who have been saved from sin will get to heaven.

The table below might help you answer such a question.

Arguments for	Arguments against
Christian teaching on atonement says that without the atonement brought by Jesus there can be no forgiveness of sins and so no entry to heaven.	Jesus said, 'Not everyone who says to me, "Lord, Lord", will enter the kingdom of heaven, but only he who does the will of my Father'.
Acts chapter 4 says that salvation can only be found in Jesus and without Jesus there can be no salvation and so no entry to heaven.	Jesus said in the Parable of the Sheep and the Goats that only those who help the hungry and homeless, etc., will enter heaven.
John's Gospel teaches that those who do not believe in God's Son will perish, but those who do believe will have eternal life.	If God is all-loving, then he will not turn away good, kind people just because they have not been saved.

Topic 1.1.6 Christian eschatology

REVISED

Eschatology refers to religious beliefs about death, judgement and life after death. Christians have different beliefs about eschatology.

- Evangelical Protestants believe in resurrection of the body – after death, the body stays in the grave until the Last Day, when Jesus will return to earth to declare the end of the world. The dead will be raised and join the living for the final judgement which will separate the good from the bad, and send the good to heaven and the bad to hell (some believe that good non-Christians will not go to hell).
- Liberal Protestants believe in **immortality of the soul** (at death the body dies, but the soul lives on in a spiritual world). They believe that all souls will be given a second chance to make it to heaven and that hell is not a real place but a separation from God. Some Liberal Protestants do not believe in hell at all.
- Catholic Christians believe that after death, the perfectly purified will go to heaven, evil people will go to hell and those with unforgiven sins go to **purgatory** where they will be purified from their sins. At the end of the world all will be raised and the souls from purgatory will join those in heaven, but the souls in hell will return there. No Protestants believe in purgatory because it is not mentioned in the Bible.

The Bible and life after death

- Belief in resurrection is taught by St Paul, especially in 1 Corinthians 15.
- Belief in immortality of the soul comes from Jesus telling the robber on the cross, 'This day you will be with me in paradise', and from Moses and Elijah appearing at Jesus' transfiguration.
- The final judgement and being sent to heaven and hell is shown most clearly in the Parable of the Sheep and the Goats.
- The Bible is full of references to heaven as the abode of God and the angels.
- St Paul in 2 Corinthians teaches that Christians long for heaven and because they are aiming for heaven, they lead good lives.

The importance of life after death for Christians

The beliefs are important because:

- Christians think that what they believe and how they live will determine what happens to them after death
- Christians believe sin can stop them getting to heaven so they try to avoid sins
- beliefs about life after death give Christians' lives meaning and purpose.

Eschatology – religious beliefs about death, judgement and life after death

Immortality of the soul – the idea that the soul lives on after the death of the body

Purgatory – a place where Catholic Christians believe souls go after death to be purified

Sources of wisdom and authority

- St Paul says in 1 Corinthians that the dead will be raised at the end of the world.
- In the Parable of the Sheep and the Goats, Jesus says that God will sort the good (those who help the suffering) from the bad (those who do not help the suffering) and send the good to heaven and the bad to hell.
- The Catechism of the Catholic Church teaches that sinful Christians will go to purgatory to be purified.

Now test yourself

TESTED

1 Beliefs about life after death are referred to as:
 a) immortality of the soul
 b) eschatology
 c) purgatory
 d) resurrection

2 The belief that at death, the body dies but the soul lives on in a spiritual world is known as:
 a) immortality of the soul
 b) eschatology
 c) purgatory
 d) resurrection

3 The belief that, after death, the body stays in the grave until the end of the world, when it is raised, is known as:
 a) immortality of the soul
 b) eschatology
 c) purgatory
 d) resurrection

4 The place where Catholics believe souls go after death to be purified is called:
 a) immortality of the soul
 b) eschatology
 c) purgatory
 d) resurrection

Activities

Complete the answers to these questions:

1 Outline three features of Catholic teaching about life after death.

The Catholic Church teaches that, after death, the perfectly purified go to heaven and evil people go to hell. Catholics with unforgiven sins go to...

2 Explain two reasons why beliefs about life after death are important for Christians. In your answer you must refer to a source of wisdom and authority.

Christians believe that what they believe and how they live will determine what happens to them after death. As Jesus said in the Parable of the Sheep and the Goats, God will sort the good (those who help the suffering) from the bad (those who do not help the suffering) and send the good to heaven and the bad to hell. Beliefs about life after death are also important for Christians because ...

Exam support

You might be asked to evaluate a statement such as:

Christians are better people because of their beliefs about life after death.

The table below might help you answer such a question.

Arguments for	Arguments against
Christians believe that what happens to them after they die will be based on how they have lived this life, so they try to live a good Christian life. Living a good Christian life means loving God and loving your neighbour as yourself. Trying to love your neighbour as yourself is bound to make Christians better people.	Surveys show that Christians do not give more to charity than non-Christians.
In the Parable of the Sheep and the Goats, Jesus said Christians should feed the hungry, clothe the naked, befriend strangers and visit the sick and those in prison.	Statistics show that there are just as many Christians in prison as non-religious people.
Jesus taught in the Good Samaritan that loving your neighbour means helping anyone in need. This is why Christians work for Christian Aid, CAFOD, etc., and do more to help other people than non-Christians.	Despite the Bible and Church teachings about divorce, statistics show that Christians have a similar level of family breakdowns (such as divorce or children in care) as non-Christians.

Topic 1.1.7 The problem of evil and suffering

REVISED

Evil and suffering can take two forms:

Moral suffering: This is suffering that is caused by humans misusing their free will (the human ability to make choices) to do something evil. War is a good example of moral evil. Wars cause large amounts of suffering, and all wars are caused by the actions of humans who could have chosen to act differently. Rape, murder and burglary are clear examples of moral suffering. Christians often call actions causing moral suffering sins because they are against what God wants humans to do (for example, they break the Ten Commandments).

Natural suffering: Natural suffering is suffering that has not been caused by humans. Earthquakes, floods, volcanoes and serious illnesses such as cancer result in lots of human suffering.

Holocaust – mass murder of the Jews by the Nazis in the Second World War

Moral suffering – suffering caused by actions done by humans

Natural suffering – suffering which is caused by nature and has nothing to do with humans

Omnibenevolent – all-good

Omnipotent – all-powerful

Omniscient – knowing everything that has happened and everything that is going to happen

How evil and suffering cause people to question or reject belief in God

Some people believe that a loving God would not have designed a world with natural evils in it. There would be no floods, earthquakes, volcanoes, cancer etc. As God must be able to do things better than humans, they believe natural evil shows God has not created the world.

Some people cannot believe in a God who allows humans to cause so much evil and suffering when he could stop it if he wanted to. God could have stopped the Second World War and the **Holocaust**. As both events happened, this may mean that God does not exist.

Why evil and suffering cause problems for Christians

- If God is **omnipotent** (all-powerful), he must be able to remove evil and suffering from the world.
- If God is **omnibenevolent** (all-good), he must want to remove evil and suffering from the world
- If God is **omniscient** (knows everything), he must have known the evil and suffering that would come from creating the universe.
- It follows that, if God exists, there should be no evil or suffering in the world.
- As there is evil and suffering in the world, either God is not all-good, or all-powerful, or all-knowing, or God does not exist.

Christians do believe that God is omnipotent, omnibenevolent and omniscient, so the existence of evil and suffering challenges their beliefs about God.

Sources of wisdom and authority

- The Psalms say that God is all-loving, his love is as high as the heavens are above the earth.
- The Book of Job and the Psalms say that God is all-powerful, he can do anything.

Now test yourself

TESTED

1 Suffering caused by actions done by humans is called:
   a) natural suffering
   b) innocent suffering
   c) evil suffering
   d) moral suffering

2 Suffering that is caused by nature and has nothing to do with humans is called:
   a) natural suffering
   b) innocent suffering
   c) evil suffering
   d) moral suffering

3 The word meaning that God is all-good is:
   a) omnibenevolent
   b) omnipotent
   c) omniscient
   d) omnipresent

4 The word meaning that God is all-powerful is called:
   a) omnibenevolent
   b) omnipotent
   c) omniscient
   d) omnipresent

5 The word meaning that God knows everything that has happened and everything that is going to happen is:
   a) omnibenevolent
   b) omnipotent
   c) omniscient
   d) omnipresent

Activities

Complete the answers to these questions:

1 Outline three features of the problem of evil and suffering for Christians.

If God is omnipotent, he must be able to get rid of evil and suffering.

If God is omnibenevolent, he must ....

If God is omniscient, he must ....

2 Explain two reasons why evil and suffering in the world cause problems for Christian beliefs about the nature of God. In your answer you must refer to a source of wisdom and authority.

The Bible teaches Christians that God will protect them from evil and suffering, and yet good Christians seem to suffer as anyone else.

The Psalms say that God is all-loving, his love is as high as the heavens are above the earth, and the Book of Job says that God is all-powerful, he can do anything. This means there should be ....

Exam support

You might be asked to evaluate a statement such as: *Evil and suffering are the fault of humans.*

The table below might help you answer such a question.

Arguments for	Arguments against
Massive amounts of suffering are caused by wars which can only be the fault of humans.	Lots of suffering is caused by earthquakes which are the result of the tectonic design of the earth.
Lots of suffering comes from criminal activity (murder, rape, arson, burglary, etc.) which can only be the fault of humans.	Much suffering is caused by hurricanes which result from the interaction of tropical seas and the earth's atmosphere.
Suffering comes from diseases which are caused by humans abusing their bodies by smoking, taking drugs, drinking alcohol and over-eating.	Suffering is caused by genetic diseases (such cystic fibrosis and Huntington's disease), as well as childhood cancers, which have nothing to do with humans' actions or behaviour.

Topic 1.1.8 Solutions to the problem of evil and suffering

REVISED

Christianity responds to the problem of evil and suffering in three main ways – biblical, theoretical and practical.

Biblical responses

- The Book of Job explains how God allowed Satan to punish sinless Job to prove to Satan that Job loved God. Job protested to God, but when he came face to face with God, he realised that God is so great that humans have no right to challenge him. God has a reason for suffering, but it is beyond human understanding.
- The Book of **Psalms** explains that suffering is simply a part of life but so is joy, and the two exist side by side. However, the Psalms also claim that suffering can bring believers to a deeper understanding of God.

Theoretical responses

- The **free will** response is the idea that God created humans in his image, which means he created them with free will. Humans therefore have the freedom to do good or evil, to believe in God or not believe in God. This freedom means that God cannot interfere if humans choose evil, and the suffering which results is the fault of humans, not God.
- The **vale of soul making** response claims that the evil and suffering involved in this life are not a problem because this life is a preparation for eternal paradise. If people are to improve their souls they need to face evil and suffering in order to become good, kind and loving. God cannot remove evil and suffering if he is going to give people the chance to become good people. But, in the end, he will show his omnibenevolence and omnipotence by rewarding the good in heaven.
- The good out of evil response, which claims that suffering may have the purpose of bringing good out of people. This is because people often respond to suffering by determining to improve things and ensuring that suffering is reduced or even removed.
- The no answer response claims that God has a reason for not using his power to remove evil and suffering, but humans cannot understand it. God is divine and there is no way humans can understand his thoughts.

Practical responses

The main Christian response to evil and suffering is to follow the example of Jesus and react in practical ways.

- Christians pray for those who are suffering, asking for God's help through **intercessionary prayers**.
- Christians also give practical help to those who suffer. Many Christians become doctors, nurses and social workers, for example, so that they can help to reduce the amount of suffering in the world.

Free will – the idea that human beings are free to make their own choices

Intercessionary prayers – prayers asking God's help for other people

Psalms – a book of the Old Testament containing 150 sacred songs

Vale of soul making – the idea that God gave people this life to make their souls good enough for heaven

Sources of wisdom and authority

- The Book of Psalms says that being afflicted by suffering leads to greater understanding of God.
- The Book of Job says God is so wonderful that his actions cannot be questioned.

Now test yourself

TESTED

1 What does the vale of soul making response claim?
   a) Suffering is justified by God because if humans are to improve their souls, they need to experience evil and suffering in order to become good people.
   b) Suffering is justified by how God rewards people in this life.
   c) Suffering is justified by God rewarding all who suffer in a future life.
   d) There is so much suffering in this life it can never be justified.

2 What is the name of the book of the Old Testament which contains 150 sacred songs?
   a) Song of Songs
   b) Ecclesiastes
   c) Lamentations
   d) Psalms

3 What are intercessionary prayers?
   a) Prayers thanking God for other people
   b) Prayers blessing the bread and wine in the Eucharist
   c) Prayers asking for God's help and guidance
   d) Prayers asking for God's help for other people

4 What is the state of being very moral and spiritual called?
   a) Sainthood
   b) Holiness
   c) Blessedness
   d) Martyrdom

Activities

Complete the answers to these questions:

1 Outline three different ways in which Christians respond to the problem of evil and suffering.

One way is by using the biblical responses such as those in the books of Job and Psalms.

A second way is the theoretical response, such as

……………………………………………………………

……………………………………………………………

A third way is a practical response, such as

……………………………………………………………

……………………………………………………………

2 Explain two biblical responses to the problem of evil and suffering. In your answer you must refer to a source of wisdom and authority.

The Book of Job explains how God allowed Satan to punish sinless Job to prove to Satan that Job loved God. Job protested to God, but when he came face to face with God, he realised that God is so great that humans have no right to challenge him. God has a reason for suffering, but it is just too complex for humans to understand.

The Book of Psalms explains that ……………………………

……………………………………………………………

Exam support

You might be asked to evaluate a statement such as: *Evil and suffering are not a problem for Christians.*

The table below might help you answer such a question.

Arguments for	Arguments against
Christians believe that an all-good, all-powerful God can allow evil and suffering, for the reasons shown below.	Atheists believe evil and suffering cannot be justified, for the reasons shown below.
The Bible shows that God must have a reason for allowing evil and suffering, but humans cannot understand it.	If God is omnipotent, he must be able to remove evil and suffering from the world. If God is omnibenevolent, he must want to remove evil and suffering from the world. So if God exists, there should be no evil or suffering in the world.
By making humans with free will, God created a world in which evil and suffering will come about through humans misusing their free will. So evil and suffering is a problem caused by humans, not God.	The world has features that are the fault of God's design (floods, earthquakes, volcanoes and serious illness). They cannot be blamed on humans and so cannot be justified.
The evil and suffering involved in this life are not a problem because this life is a preparation for paradise, which will justify all the suffering.	An all-powerful God could stop evil humans from causing so much suffering, and his not doing so cannot be justified.
God has a reason for not using his power to remove evil and suffering, but humans cannot understand it. God is divine and so humans cannot understand his thoughts.	If God is omniscient, he would have known the evil and suffering that would come from creating this universe and so he should have created a different universe with no suffering.

1.2 Marriage and the family

Topic 1.2.1 Marriage

REVISED

Christian attitudes to marriage

Christians believe that marriage:

- was created by God at the beginning of the world so that a couple can have a **lifelong relationship** of love and **faithfulness**
- should be between one man and one woman (**monogamy**)
- is the only acceptable way for Christians to have sexual relationships
- is the way for Christians to have children and start a family
- is the way new life is brought into the Church through Christian families
- was established by God to preserve society.

For Catholic and Orthodox Christians, marriage is one of the seven sacraments.

Humanist and atheist attitudes to marriage

All Humanists and many atheists believe that it is up to the individual whether they marry or just live together (**cohabit**), but relationships should be exclusive (only one partner at a time). Many marry because it gives the relationship more stability and legal protection, especially if children are involved.

Changing attitudes

Most people now have sex before marriage, and most couples cohabit before they marry. Marriage is no longer seen as for life as divorce is now accepted. Marriage is no longer seen as religious as most weddings are not held in church.

Christian responses to changing attitudes

The official response of Catholic and Conservative Protestant Churches has been to condemn pre-marital sex, cohabitation and same-sex marriage.

The official response of Liberal Protestant Churches has been to accept the new attitudes to marriage, but encourage Christians to marry, especially if they want to start a family.

Many Christians, especially younger ones, ignore the official teachings and accept the new attitudes.

Sources of wisdom and authority

- Jesus said that marriage was created by God at the beginning.
- Jesus says in Mark's Gospel that husband and wife are joined by God and should not be separated.

Cohabitation – living as man and wife without being married

Faithfulness – staying with your marriage partner and having sex only with them

Lifelong relationship – the idea that marriage can only be ended by the death of a partner

Monogamy – marriage to only one person at a time

Now test yourself

TESTED

1 Christians believe that marriage was:
 a) commanded by God in the Torah
 b) created by God at the beginning of the world
 c) commanded by Jesus in the Gospels
2 Marriage is one of the seven sacraments for:
 a) Catholic Christians
 b) Baptist Christians
 c) Methodist Christians
3 Humanists and atheists:
 a) do not believe in marriage
 b) think living together is better than marriage
 c) think sex and marriage are up to the individual
4 Marriage to only one person at the same time is known as:
 a) bigamy
 b) polygamy
 c) monogamy

Activities

Complete the answers to these questions:

1 Outline three Christian beliefs about marriage.

Christians believe that marriage was created by God at the beginning of the world. They believe that marriage is for a couple to have a lifelong relationship of love. They also believe that marriage is

....

2 Explain two reasons why Christians get married. In your answer you must refer to a source of wisdom and authority.

Christians get married because, for many Christians, marriage is one of the seven sacraments. It is therefore a sign of grace, instituted by Christ himself, and, through the Church, imparting God's grace and strength. Christians believe they should take part in the sacraments if at all possible and so they feel they should marry. They should also marry because Jesus said that ....

Exam support

You might be asked to evaluate a statement such as:

Couples don't need to marry to have a happy relationship.

The table below might help you answer such a question.

Arguments for	Arguments against
Couples who live together can be just as happy and committed as those who marry.	Marriage is God's gift (a sacrament for many Christians) and the way humans should have sex and raise a family.
You can't promise to stay with someone until death if you don't know what it will be like to live with them.	The Bible teaches that sex should only take place in marriage and that marriage is necessary for the upbringing of a Christian family.
Living together brings all the commitment and joy of marriage without the legal complications.	The Church teaches that marriage is the basis of society and that living together without marriage is wrong.
Weddings are expensive and living together allows a couple to spend that money on the home, children, etc.	Statistics show that married couples are more likely to stay together than cohabiting couples and that the children of married couples have a more stable and happier life.

Topic 1.2.2 Sexual relationships

REVISED

Christianity teaches that sex is a gift from God to be enjoyed between one man and one woman who are married to each other, and for the procreation of children.

Christian teachings about sexual relationships outside of marriage

Most Christians are opposed to **pre-marital sex** because it is condemned by the Bible and Church teachings such as the Catechism of the Catholic Church.

All Christians are against **adultery** (also known as extra-marital sex) because it breaks the wedding vows and is condemned in the Ten Commandments and by Jesus in the Gospels.

Humanist and atheist attitudes to sexual relationships

Humanists and non-religious people accept sex before marriage and **cohabitation** because they believe that sexual relationships should be the choice of the people involved. They think that sex should be **consensual**, be between people 'of age', and should not involve cheating on a partner.

Christian attitudes to same-sex relationships

The various changes in the laws on **homosexuality** have led to a greater acceptance of equal rights for homosexuals. There are differing Christian attitudes to homosexuality:

- The Catholic Church teaches that being a homosexual is not a sin, but homosexual sexual relationships are a sin. The Church does not accept same-sex marriage, but is less opposed to **civil partnerships** and teaches that it is sinful to harass homosexuals or attack their behaviour (**homophobia**). The reasons for this view are:
    - the Bible condemns homosexual sexual activity
    - the Church teaches that sexual activity should be creative as well as unitive (see Topic 1.2.5) and homosexuals cannot have procreative sex
- Evangelical Protestants believe that homosexuality is a sin. They do not accept same-sex marriage and believe that the power of the Spirit can change people's sexual preference (orientation). They believe this because the Bible condemns homosexuality.
- Liberal Protestants believe that lifelong homosexual relationships are acceptable. They have homosexual ministers and priests, and provide blessings for civil partnerships because they feel the Bible reflects ideas of the time rather than God's will.

Non-religious attitudes to same-sex relationships

Humanists, and the vast majority of non-religious people, see no problems with sexual relations between homosexuals.

Christian responses to the non-religious attitudes

- Roman Catholic and Evangelical Protestant Churches have condemned the non-religious attitude and insisted that homosexual Christians should refrain from all sexual activity and ban same-sex marriages.
- Liberal Protestants have welcomed homosexuals into the Church, but will not perform same-sex marriages in church.

Adultery – a sexual act between a married person and someone other than their marriage partner

Civil partnerships – legal ceremonies giving homosexual partners the same legal rights as husband and wife

Cohabitation – living together in a sexual relationship without being married

Consensual sex – when both parties freely agree to sexual activity

Homophobia – hatred or fear of homosexuals

Homosexuality – sexual attraction to someone of the same sex

Pre-marital sex – sexual activity before marriage

Sources of wisdom and authority

- The Catechism says that sex must only take place within marriage.
- St Paul said that homosexuals will never enter heaven.

Now test yourself

TESTED

1 Sex before marriage is known as:
   a) cohabitation
   b) consensual sex
   c) pre-marital sex
   d) extra-marital sex
2 A couple living together in a sexual relationship without being married is known as:
   a) cohabitation
   b) consensual sex
   c) pre-marital sex
   d) extra-marital sex
3 A sexual relationship between a married person and someone other than their marriage partner is:
   a) cohabitation
   b) consensual sex
   c) pre-marital sex
   d) extra-marital sex

Activities

Complete the answers to these questions:

1 Outline three Christian beliefs about sexual relationships.

Christians believe sex is a gift from God. They believe that pre-marital sex is wrong and they also believe that ....

2 Explain two reasons why some Christians are against same-sex relationships. In your answer you must refer to a source of wisdom and authority.

Evangelical Protestants believe that homosexuality is a sin. They do not accept same-sex marriage and believe that the Bible condemns homosexuality. They believe that the salvation of Christ can remove all sins, including homosexuality, so there is no need for same-sex relationships.

St Paul said that homosexuals will never enter heaven.

The Catholic Church teaches that ....

Exam support

You might be asked to evaluate a statement such as: *Same-sex marriage is wrong.*

The table below might help you answer such a question.

Arguments for	Arguments against
Christianity teaches that God gave marriage for a man and a woman, not two people of the same-sex.	A same-sex marriage allows homosexual couples to commit themselves to each other and encourages stable sexual relationships.
One of the purposes of Christian marriage is for the procreation of children and as homosexuals cannot procreate, they cannot marry.	Same-sex marriages are part of giving homosexuals equal rights.
Christians who believe homosexuals should not be sexually active cannot accept same-sex marriages because they encourage homosexual sexual activity.	Same-sex marriages allow homosexual couples to share their belongings, pensions, etc., in just the same way as heterosexual couples.
Most Christian clergy (priests or ministers) will not bless same-sex marriages.	Same-sex marriages are a way of encouraging the Christian virtues of love and faithfulness among homosexuals.

Topic 1.2.3 Families

REVISED

The nature of families

Human children cannot survive on their own until they approach adulthood and so the family unit has developed. The main family types are:

- Nuclear families – mother, father and children living together as a unit.
- Single parent families – children living with only one of their parents.
- Same-sex parent families – families which are headed by two men or two women. The Equality Act 2010 made discriminating against same-sex couples illegal and gave them equal adoption and fostering rights.
- Extended families – three generations (parents, children and grandparents) living in the same house or in close proximity and having frequent contact and reliance on each other.
- Blended families – two separate families joined together by a parent from one family marrying a parent from the other family. The increase in divorce has led to an increase in **remarriage** and so there are now more blended families.

The purpose and importance of the family in Christianity

All Christians believe that Christian parents have a duty to:

- ensure that the **physical needs** and **material needs** of the children are met
- instil **moral values** into their children so that they become good and responsible citizens
- bring the children up in the Christian faith and do their best to ensure that the children become Christian adults.

Family life is important for Christians because one of the main purposes of Christian marriage is to have children and bring them up in a secure and loving Christian environment so that they will come to love God and follow Jesus. The family is the place where children learn the difference between right and wrong. It is also the place where children are introduced to the faith and so is very important for Christianity to continue and grow.

Material needs – such things as food, drink and clothing

Moral values – the standards of good and evil, which influence people's behaviour and choices

Physical needs – such things as housing and shelter from the elements

Remarriage – marrying again after a divorce

Different Christian attitudes to the family

Some Christians believe that the purpose of the family is to make sure that children are educated to think for themselves so that they can make up their own minds about religion when they are old enough.

Sources of wisdom and authority

- One of the Ten Commandments says that you should honour your parents.
- St Paul said that parents should bring their children up in the way of the Lord.

Now test yourself

TESTED

1 Food, drink and clothing are:
   a) physical needs
   b) essential needs
   c) material needs
   d) daily needs
2 Housing and shelter from the elements are:
   a) physical needs
   b) essential needs
   c) material needs
   d) daily needs
3 The standards of good and evil, which govern people's behaviour and choices, are known as:
   a) social values
   b) community values
   c) religious values
   d) moral values
4 Two separate families joined together by a parent from one family marrying a parent from the other family are described as:
   a) a nuclear family
   b) an extended family
   c) a single parent family
   d) a blended family

Activities

Complete the answers to these questions:

1 Outline three types of family.

A nuclear family is a mother, father and children living together as a unit.

A second type of family is ....

A third type of family is ....

2 Explain two reasons why the family is important to Christians. In your answer, you must refer to a source of wisdom and authority.

The family is important to Christians because one of the main purposes of Christian marriage is to have children. St Paul said that parents should bring up their children in the way of the Lord.

The family is also important for Christians because it is the place where children are introduced to the Christian faith through ....

Exam support

You might be asked to evaluate a statement such as:

The family is more important for Christians than for non-religious people.

The table below might help you answer such a question.

Arguments for	Arguments against
One of the main purposes of Christian marriage is to have children and bring them up in a secure and loving Christian environment so that they will come to love God and follow Jesus.	Many non-religious people see their family as being the most important thing in their lives, whereas many religious people see their religion as more important than their family.
Christians are taught that the family was created by God as the basic unit of society.	Most non-religious people have just as good a family life as religious people.
A Christian family is the place where children are introduced to the faith and so it is very important for Christianity to continue and grow.	Non-religious families may respect their children more because they don't try to insist they be religious.
Christians believe that God will judge them on how well they have raised their family.	Religion cannot make a difference to how much love parents feel for their children and vice versa.

Topic 1.2.4 Support for the family in the local parish

REVISED

What is the parish?

The organisation of the Roman Catholic and Anglican Churches is based on parishes and **dioceses**. A parish is an area around a local church and has a **parish priest** (usually known as a **vicar** in the Church of England). A diocese is a collection of parishes under the control of a **bishop**.

How the parish tries to help families

- Most Catholic or Church of England parishes have a local Church primary and secondary school connected to them, providing Christian education and worship in addition to the standard education. This education teaches children about the Christian faith and choosing right from wrong.
- Many churches are developing family-friendly worship to strengthen families. Family worship helps to unite the family and gives families an opportunity to discover religion together.
- Most parish **clergy** are available for help with family and marital problems, and many Church of England dioceses have a Children and Family Officer.
- Most churches run toddler groups, youth clubs and youth activities such as Girls Brigade and Boys Brigade, which help parents to bring up their children as good Christians.

Bishop – specially chosen priest who is responsible for all the churches in a diocese

Clergy – those ordained by the Church

Diocese – a Church area under the direction of a bishop

Parish priest/vicar – the clergy person responsible for a local church

Why parishes try to help families

- Parishes try to help families because they have a duty to help children baptised or dedicated in the Church.
- The Church teaches that one of the main purposes of Christian marriage is to have children and bring them up to love God and follow Jesus, so it is the responsibility of the parish to assist in that task.
- Christians believe the family is the most important part of society and without the family society would collapse, so the parish has a social as well as sacred duty to help parents with their family life.
- If the parish does not help the family, then Christianity will not grow.

Why support from the Church is important for Christian families

- Raising children as Christians means taking them to church regularly and that requires the church to be helpful to children.
- Teaching children about Christianity requires knowledge and expertise in the faith that parents are not likely to have, so Church schools and Sunday Schools are able to provide that support.
- For Catholic, Anglican and Orthodox families, taking part in the sacraments is essential and that requires the help of the Church.

Sources of wisdom and authority

- Jesus said that children should be allowed to come to him because the kingdom of heaven belongs to children.
- In the baptism service Methodists promise to help in the upbringing of children.

Now test yourself

TESTED

1 Who is responsible for all the churches in a diocese?
   a) A vicar
   b) A parish priest
   c) A bishop
   d) The Pope
2 What name is given to those who have been ordained by the Church?
   a) Ministers
   b) Deacons
   c) Clergy
   d) Priests
3 Who is responsible for a parish church?
   a) The bishop
   b) The parish priest
   c) The deacon
   d) The clergy

Activities

Complete the answers to these questions:

1 Outline three ways in which local parishes help families.

Most Catholic or Church of England parishes have a local Church primary and secondary school connected to them, which provides Christian education and worship as well as standard education.

Another way is ....

A third way is ....

2 Explain two reasons why parishes help families. In your answer, you must refer to a source of wisdom and authority.

Parishes try to help families because they have a duty to help children baptised or dedicated in the Church.

Jesus said ....

Another reason is ....

Exam support

You might be asked to evaluate a statement such as: *Christian parishes help to keep families together.*

The table below might help you answer such a question.

Arguments for	Arguments against
Many churches support Church schools which provide Christian education and worship in addition to the standard education.	Statistics show that Christian families are just as likely to break up as other families.
Most parish clergy are available for help with family or marital problems and dioceses have a Children and Family Officer.	Not all Christian churches provide the same level of support; some have few family-centred activities and no youth activities.
Most church services include prayers for families and for spiritual strength for parents to fulfil their responsibilities.	Some Christian churches will not provide support for families who have lapsed from the faith or have issues such as needing infertility treatments, as these are banned by the Church.
Most churches run groups such as toddler and youth clubs to help parents to bring up their children as good Christians.	

Topic 1.2.5 Family planning

REVISED

The purpose of contraception

Contraception allows couples to control the number of children they have by allowing sex to happen without conception occurring. It is estimated that 90 per cent of the sexually active population of childbearing age in the UK use some form of contraception.

- **Artificial methods of contraception:** These are the most popular and effective methods of contraception and either prevent the sperm from meeting the egg (**condoms** and diaphragms); stop a woman producing eggs (contraceptive pills and implants); or stop the fertilised egg from staying in the womb (an **IUD** or the morning-after pill). Artificial methods can be used without much planning, and in any form of sexual relationship, however casual.
- **Natural methods of contraception:** **NFP** (natural family planning) involves reducing the woman's chance of becoming pregnant by planning sex around the most infertile times during her monthly cycle.

Abortifacient – bringing about a very early abortion

Condoms – thin rubber sheath protecting against conception and STD

HIV/AIDS – if left untreated, HIV (human immunodeficiency virus) can lead to the disease known as AIDS (acquired immunodeficiency syndrome)

IUD – intra uterine device (the coil)

NFP – natural family planning

STD – sexually transmitted disease

Christian attitudes to contraception

The Catholic Church teaches that God gave sex as a source of joy and pleasure to married couples (the unitive purpose) as well as a means of creating a family (the creative purpose). This means that artificial methods are against God's intentions because:

- they separate the unitive and creative aspects of sex
- Pope Paul VI stated that the only allowable forms of contraception for Catholics are natural methods
- some contraceptives have **abortifacient** effects and so are against the teaching of the Church
- the Catholic Church regards contraception as a major cause of sexual promiscuity, broken families, the rise in the divorce rate and sexually transmitted diseases (**STDs**).

Almost all non-Catholic Christians believe that all forms of contraception are permissible because:

- Christianity is about love and justice, and contraception improves women's health and raises the standard of living of children, since families are smaller
- God created sex for enjoyment and to cement the bonds of marriage and it is not wrong to separate this from making children
- there is nothing in the Bible that forbids the use of contraception
- it is better to combat STDs such as **HIV/AIDS** by using condoms than by expecting everyone to follow Christian rules about sex and marriage.

Sources of wisdom and authority

- The Baptist Church says that contraception is a gift from God via medical science but Christians should avoid contraceptives which take life.
- The Catholic Catechism says that contraceptives which make procreation impossible are evil.
- The British Humanist Association says that contraception is a good thing because it makes every child a wanted child.

Non-religious attitudes to contraception

Non-religious people (Humanists and atheists) are in favour of all forms of contraception because they assess the rights and wrongs of birth control by looking at its consequences. They argue that because contraception prevents unwanted children from being born, improves the standard of living in families and prevents the spread of sexually transmitted diseases, it must be morally right to use it. They think contraception should be used in casual sex because it is important to avoid unwanted pregnancies and sexually transmitted diseases.

Now test yourself

TESTED

1 Which of these methods of contraception are Catholics allowed to use?
   a) Condoms
   b) IUD
   c) NFP
   d) Contraceptive pill
2 Which of these is *not* a benefit of artificial contraception?
   a) Improvements to women's health
   b) Decrease in the number of divorces
   c) Improvements to children's standard of living
   d) Decrease in sexually transmitted diseases
3 Why do non-Catholic Christians allow all forms of contraception?
   a) Artificial methods of contraception are banned by the Catholic Church
   b) Contraception is not mentioned in the Bible
   c) Contraception puts people off casual sex
   d) Artificial methods of contraception have always been allowed by the Churches
4 Why does the Catholic Church oppose artificial methods of contraception?
   a) They are banned in the Bible
   b) They prevent the true purpose of sex
   c) They separate the two purposes of sex
   d) They are banned in the creeds

Activities

Complete the answers to these questions:

1 Outline three reasons why Humanists are in favour of all methods of contraception.

Humanists are in favour of all methods of contraception because they prevent unwanted babies from being born. Another reason is ....

A third reason is ....

2 Explain two reasons why Catholic Christians are against using artificial methods of contraception. In your answer you must refer to a source of wisdom and authority.

Catholic Christians are against using artificial methods of contraception as they believe it is against God's intentions. Pope Paul VI condemned all forms of artificial methods of contraception. The Catholic Catechism says that ....

Catholics believe these methods of contraception are wrong because they separate ....

....

Exam support

You might be asked to evaluate a statement such as:

The world would be a better place if everyone followed Catholic teachings on contraception.

The table below might help you answer such a question.

Arguments for	Arguments against
Catholic teachings encourage people to restrict sex to married couples only and avoid casual sex.	Artificial methods of contraception make the world a better place because they improve women's health and well-being.
Restricting sex to married couples would reduce rates of STDs.	Contraception reduces family size and helps to raise children's standards of living.
Catholic teachings are what God wants and doing what God wants makes the world a better place.	Using contraception reduces unintended pregnancies and therefore the number of abortions.
Following Catholic teachings could reduce the number of broken families and slow the rise in the divorce rate.	Contraception provides protection against STDs including HIV and also reduces the number of pregnancies among women living with HIV, resulting in fewer infected babies and orphans.

Topic 1.2.6 Divorce and remarriage

REVISED

There has been an increase in divorce in the last 50 years, probably because new laws made divorce much cheaper and easier to obtain and equal rights legislation meant many women were financially independent and could afford to live well after a divorce. Despite this increase, 58 per cent of marriages today are unlikely to end in divorce.

Christian teachings on divorce

The Catholic Church does not allow religious divorce or remarriage. The only way a marriage between baptised Catholics can be ended is by the death of one of the partners. However, the Catholic Church does allow **civil divorce** if that will be better for the children, but the couple are still married in the eyes of God and so cannot remarry. The reasons for this attitude are:

- Jesus taught that divorce is wrong
- the couple have made a covenant with God in the **sacrament** of marriage and this 'cannot be broken by any earthly power'
- the Catechism teaches that a marriage cannot be dissolved and so religious divorce is impossible
- there can be no remarriage as there can be no religious divorce, and so remarriage would be both bigamy (having two husbands/wives) and adultery.

If it can be proved that the marriage was never a true Christian marriage, Catholics can have an **annulment** which makes them free to remarry.

Most non-Catholic Churches think that divorce is wrong, but allow it if the marriage has broken down and allow divorced people to remarry. They are sometimes asked to promise that this time their marriage will be for life. Non-Catholic Churches allow divorce because:

- Jesus allowed divorce for a partner's adultery in Matthew 19
- if a marriage has really broken down then the effects of the couple not divorcing would be a greater evil than the evil of divorce itself
- if Christians repent and confess their sins they can be forgiven. This means a couple should have another chance at marriage if they are keen to make it work this time.

Atheist and Humanist attitudes to divorce and remarriage

Atheists do not believe in God and view marriage as a purely human institution, so they allow divorce. Some atheists do not believe in marriage and instead cohabit, so would have no need to divorce.

Humanists believe that all married couples should have the right to divorce if they feel the marriage has failed. Divorce should make sure that the **spouses** are treated equally in the financial arrangements and that any children are well provided for. They believe any divorced person should be treated as a single person and so have the right to remarry if they so wish.

Annulment – a declaration by the Church that a marriage was never a true marriage and so the partners are free to marry

Civil divorce – a divorce according to the law of the country but not the Church

Sacrament – an outward ceremony through which God's grace is given

Spouse – marriage/cohabitation partner

Sources of wisdom and authority

- Jesus says in Matthew's Gospel that divorce is wrong unless one of the partners has been unfaithful.
- Jesus says in Mark's Gospel that if someone divorces and then remarries, they are committing adultery
- St Paul said that men must not divorce and if women are divorced they must remain unmarried.

Now test yourself

TESTED

1 Civil divorce is:
  a) a divorce agreed to by husband and wife
  b) a divorce allowed by the Church
  c) a divorce that only applies in one country
  d) a divorce according to the law of the country

2 Annulment is:
  a) a declaration by the Church that a couple are legally divorced
  b) a declaration by the Church that a couple can remarry
  c) a declaration by the Church that a marriage was never a true marriage
  d) a declaration by the Church that a marriage can never end

3 The Catholic Church does not allow divorce because:
  a) marriage was ordained by God
  b) divorce is condemned in the Bible
  c) marriage is a sacrament
  d) divorce has never been allowed by the Church

4 Non-Catholic Christians allow divorce because:
  a) they think it is a good thing
  b) they think it is often the lesser of two evils
  c) they think it was commanded by Jesus
  d) divorce has always been allowed by the Church

Activities

Complete the answers to these questions:

1 Outline three reasons why there has been an increase in the number of divorces.

There has been an increase in the number of divorces because of changes to the law.

Another reason is ....

A third reason is ....

2 Explain two reasons why remarriage is a problem for Catholic Christians. In your answer you must refer to a source of wisdom and authority.

Remarriage is a problem because Catholic Christians believe that a Christian marriage cannot be ended except by the death of one of the spouses. They believe that marriage is a ....

....

Catholic Christians also believe that Jesus condemned divorce and remarriage when he said ....

....

Exam support

You might be asked to evaluate a statement such as: *It is better to divorce than live in conflict.*

The table below might help you answer such a question.

Arguments for	Arguments against
It brings domestic peace and emotional security as it removes the conflict between the spouses.	It is expensive – apart from the legal costs, divorce usually means selling the family home and it is more expensive for two people to live separately than live together. The expense usually means that divorce reduces a family's living standards.
It gives opportunities for the spouses to gain personal fulfilment as they are not being forced to stay in an unhappy relationship.	It can hurt children as they are forced to choose between parents and choose which one to live with.
It reduces or ends children's exposure to damaging parental conflict since research shows it is unhealthy for children to be around parents who fight and criticise each other.	It hurts family relatives as they can often lose contact with the children if their relation is not awarded custody.
It gives people a fresh start and the chance to form new, better relationships.	It causes stress as it results in new relationships and new living situations.

Topic 1.2.7 Equality of men and women in the family

REVISED

Biblical teachings

- Genesis 1 teaches the equality of men and women as they were created at the same time and were both created in the image of God. Genesis 2–3 say that woman was created after man and out of man's rib – therefore woman is **subordinate** to man. They also explain that evil came into the world because woman persuaded man to eat the fruit of the tree which God had forbidden. As a result of this action, God allowed husbands to rule over wives.
- St Paul says in Ephesians that wives should submit to their husbands as the husband is head of the wife in the same way that Christ is head of the Church. This implies that the wife should do as she is told by the husband, but a husband should look after his wife as he looks after his own body.

So the biblical teaching of Genesis 1 says that men and women should have equal roles in life because they were created equal. However, Genesis 2–3 and Ephesians say that men have the **dominant role**.

Dominant role – the major, most influential part

Equalists – those who believe in, and practise, the complete equality of men and women

Subordinate – of inferior importance or rank

Suffragettes – women who campaigned for the right to vote in the early twentieth century

Christian attitudes to equal roles of men and women

- Many Evangelical Protestants teach that it is the role of women to bring up children and run a Christian home. Women should not speak in church and must cover their heads and must submit to their husbands. It is the role of men to provide for the family and to lead the family in religion as only men can be church leaders and teachers. This attitude is based on St Paul's teaching that the husband is the head of the wife, the teaching of Genesis 2 about Adam being created first and the disciples of Jesus being men.
- Liberal Protestants believe that men and women are equal and should have equal roles. This is based on the teachings of Genesis 1 that male and female were created at the same time and equally, the teaching of St Paul in Galatians that in Christ there is neither male nor female and the evidence from the Gospels that Jesus treated women as his equals.
- The Catholic Church teaches that men and women should have equal roles in life and the family. In accordance with Genesis 1:27, the Church teaches that men and women have equal status in the sight of God, although Catholic women cannot have equal roles in the Church because only men can be priests.
- In the new Roman Catholic marriage service, the priest says: 'May her husband put his trust in her and recognise that she is his equal and the heir with him to the life of grace.'

Sources of wisdom and authority

- Genesis says that God created male and female in his own image.
- St Paul says in 1 Timothy that women should not teach or speak in church.
- St Paul says in Ephesians that wives should submit to their husbands because the husband is the head of the wife, just as Christ is the head of the Church.
- St Paul says in Galatians 3 that in Christ there is neither male nor female.

Atheist and Humanist attitudes to equal roles of men and women in the family

Atheists believe that men and women are equal and should have equal roles in the family.

Humanists base their beliefs on science and reason and so most Humanists would say they are **equalists**, that is they believe that men and women are equal and should have equal rights and therefore equal roles in the family. Many of the **suffragettes** and early feminists were Humanists.

Now test yourself

TESTED

1 St Paul says in Galatians 3 that:
   a) men and women are equal
   b) wives should submit to their husbands
   c) in Christ there is neither male nor female
   d) woman was created out of man, so woman is subordinate to man
2 Genesis 1 says that:
   a) men and women are equal
   b) wives should submit to their husbands
   c) in Christ there is neither male nor female
   d) woman was created out of man, so woman is subordinate to man
3 St Paul says in Ephesians that:
   a) men and women are equal
   b) wives should submit to their husbands
   c) in Christ there is neither male nor female
   d) woman was created out of man, so woman is subordinate to man
4 Genesis 2–3 say that:
   a) men and women are equal
   b) wives should submit to their husbands
   c) in Christ there is neither male nor female
   d) woman was created out of man, so woman is subordinate to man

Activities

Complete the answers to these questions:

1 Outline two reasons why some Christians think men and women should have different roles in the family.

Some Christians think they should have different roles because it is what Genesis teaches in the story of Adam and Eve. St Paul says in Ephesians ....

2 Explain two reason why some Christians believe that men and women should have equal roles in the family. In your answer you must refer to a source of wisdom and authority.

Liberal Protestants believe that men and women are equal, and should have equal roles. This is based on the teachings of Genesis that ....

Liberal Protestants also believe that St Paul taught the equality of the sexes when he said ....

....

Exam support

You might be asked to evaluate a statement such as:

Christian families do not treat women equally.

The table below might help you answer such a question.

Arguments for	Arguments against
Many Evangelical Protestants teach that it is the role of women to bring up children and run a Christian home.	Liberal Protestants believe that men and women are equal, and should have equal roles in the family and life.
They believe women should dress simply and submit to their husbands.	The Catholic Church teaches that men and women should have equal roles in life and the family.
Evangelical Protestants believe it is the role of men to provide for the family and to lead the family in religion as only men can be church leaders and teachers.	Genesis 1 teaches that male and female were created at the same time and equally.
Genesis 2 says men are superior because Adam was created first.	St Paul says in Galatians that in Christ there is neither male nor female.

Topic 1.2.8 Gender prejudice and discrimination

REVISED

Christian teachings about gender prejudice and discrimination

There are three different Christian attitudes to gender prejudice and discrimination:

- Evangelical Protestants teach that men and women have separate and different roles and so cannot have equal rights in religion. They believe that women should not speak in church, should not teach and must submit to their husbands. It is the role of men to provide for the family and to lead the family in religion.
- The Catholic Church is against **gender prejudice** and **gender discrimination** and the **Catholic Catechism** teaches that men and women are equal. However, only men can be **ordained** since it is the special function of the priest to represent Jesus at the Mass, the **apostles** were all men, and priests and bishops are successors of the apostles. Women are able to become **extraordinary ministers**, which enables them to assist the work of priests.
- Liberal Protestant Churches believe that men and women should have totally equal roles in life and the family. They have women ministers, priests and bishops because Genesis 1 says that God created male and female at the same time and of equal status.

Apostle – one chosen by Jesus to preach his gospel (often used for the twelve disciples)

Catholic Catechism – the official teaching of the Roman Catholic Church

Extraordinary minister – a non-ordained man or woman who assists the work of priests

Gender discrimination – putting gender prejudice into practice and treating people differently because of their sex

Gender equality – the sexes being treated equally

Gender prejudice – believing that one sex is superior to another, based on feeling rather than an assessment of evidence

Ordained – made a priest

Ordination – the act of conferring holy orders (making a priest)

Sexism – discrimination, prejudice or stereotyping on the basis of gender

Christian opposition to gender prejudice and discrimination

The Movement for the Ordination of Women (MOW) believed that the Church of England's refusal to have women priests was gender discrimination. The group campaigned for the **ordination** of women and after twenty years of struggle, the first women priests in the Church of England were ordained at Bristol Cathedral in 1993.

Another group of Christian men and women, Women and the Church, continued the fight for **gender equality** in the Church of England. However, it was not until 2013 that the first woman bishop in the Church of England was ordained (there had been women priests and bishops much earlier in the American and Canadian Anglican Churches).

Women's Ordination Worldwide (WOW) is a network of groups whose mission is to end gender discrimination and persuade the Vatican to allow Catholic women to become priests. In September 2015, however, Pope Francis said, 'women priests, that cannot be done. Pope St John Paul II after long, long intense discussions, long reflection, said so clearly'.

Sources of wisdom and authority

- The Catechism says that only men can be priests because Jesus only chose men as his apostles.
- St Paul's letters show that he had women helpers he considered as equals.
- St Paul says in 1 Timothy that women should not teach or have authority over men.

Atheist and Humanist attitudes to gender prejudice and discrimination

Most atheists and all Humanists believe that men and women are equal and should have equal rights. Humanists are against **sexism** and have been keen supporters of legislation to promote women's rights. Humanists believe that it is wrong for religion to discriminate against women and that refusing to ordain women or have women leaders should be made illegal.

Now test yourself

TESTED

1. Gender prejudice is:
   a) believing that one sex is superior to another, based on feelings rather than evidence
   b) believing the sexes are equal
   c) treating people differently because of their sex
   d) stereotyping on the basis of gender
2. Gender discrimination is:
   a) believing that one sex is superior to another, based on feelings rather than evidence
   b) believing the sexes are equal
   c) treating people differently because of their sex
   d) stereotyping on the basis of gender
3. The act of making a priest is called:
   a) sanctification
   b) sacramentation
   c) ordination
   d) elevation
4. An extraordinary minister is:
   a) a priest with special powers
   b) a woman who is allowed to do some of the tasks of a priest
   c) a non-ordained person who can fulfil the role of a priest
   d) a non-ordained person who assists the work of priests

Activities

Complete the answers to these questions:

1 Outline three roles of ministry that Catholic women are able to perform.

Catholic women are allowed to study and teach in theological colleges. They can also ....

....

Catholic women can also ....

2 Explain two reasons why Christians have different attitudes to gender prejudice and discrimination. In your answer you must refer to a source of wisdom and authority.

Liberal Protestants oppose gender prejudice and discrimination because they believe that men and women are equal, and should have equal roles in life and in the Church. They have women priests and ministers because St Paul had women helpers who he treated as equals and there is evidence that Jesus treated women as his equals.

Evangelical Protestants believe that ....

Exam support

You might be asked to evaluate a statement such as:

Christians should never treat women differently from men.

The table below might help you answer such a question.

Arguments for	Arguments against
Genesis 1 says that God created male and female at the same time and of equal status.	Genesis 2–3 say that Adam was created first and it was the woman who led man astray.
St Paul teaches in Galatians that men and women are of equal status.	St Paul teaches in 1 Timothy that women should not speak in church and should not teach.
The Gospels show that Jesus treated women as his equals.	St Paul teaches in Ephesians that women must submit to their husbands.
Liberal Christian Churches say it is wrong to treat women differently.	The Catholic Church teaches that women cannot have equal rights in the Church. They cannot be priests because Jesus was a man and chose men to be his apostles.

1.3 Living the Christian life

Topic 1.3.1 Worship

REVISED

There are different forms of worship just as there are different Churches in Christianity.

- **Liturgical worship** is public worship in church that uses a service book with set prayers and rituals so that everything follows the same format. The set form of the **liturgy** means that rituals have developed to help the worshippers to feel closer to God, people can join in at set points and the words are familiar. The **clergy** usually wear special **vestments**. Worship follows the **liturgical year** which begins at Advent, and follows through Christmas, Epiphany, Lent, Easter and Pentecost. The readings follow a three-year cycle and are set out in a **lectionary** which enables **congregations** to hear most of the Bible read every three years. Liturgical worship is the main form of worship in Roman Catholic, Orthodox and many Anglican Churches, but is only used for Holy Communion, baptism, marriage and funerals in Protestant Churches.
- **Non-liturgical worship** is public worship in church without set prayers or rituals. The leader of the worship is free to choose the hymns, prayers and Bible readings and the main focus of the service is the sermon which can be on a theme of the leader's choice. Music in the form of hymns is often a major part of non-liturgical worship. Prayers are **extempore** (without preparation) rather than following a set form, though they usually include thanksgiving, confession and intercession, as all liturgical services do. In Pentecostal-type churches, there will often be more congregational participation and modern music.
- **Informal worship** is the type of worship many Christian families have at home such as saying grace before meals, having family prayers and celebrating the festivals of the Christian year. Many churches also have public worship in much more informal ways especially for families and young people, such as 'Messy Church'.
- **Private worship** is when Christians have the opportunity to talk to God and think about their faith by praying in private, or reading the Bible on their own.

It is important to have different types of worship because:

- public worship gives a sense of belonging to a whole community of believers
- liturgical worship helps Christians worship God in a familiar way so that worship becomes a part of their lives.
- non-liturgical worship helps to reflect people's moods, from joy to sadness, so that the worship is coming from their own feelings
- worshipping as a family brings the family together
- private worship allows people to communicate with God one to one and express emotions they cannot express in front of others
- informal worship helps people to see God in the ordinary and to realise that worship can happen anywhere in any way
- worshipping at set times gives order and purpose and means that God is never forgotten.

Clergy – people ordained for religious duties in Christian Churches

Congregation – the people assembled for worship

Extempore prayers – prayers said without preparation

Lectionary – a list of Bible readings to be read at certain times of the year

Liturgical year – the year in the Church's calendar based on the special festivals from Advent to Pentecost

Liturgy – a set form of public worship

Vestments – official robes for those leading Christian worship

Sources of wisdom and authority

- Jesus said that Christians should love God with all their heart and with all their soul, mind and strength.
- The letter to the Hebrews says that Christians should worship God with reverence and awe.

Now test yourself

TESTED

1 People ordained for religious duties in Christian Churches are known as:
   a) vicars
   b) ministers
   c) clergy
   d) pastors
2 The people assembled for worship are known as the:
   a) church
   b) body of Christ
   c) people of God
   d) congregation
3 A list of Bible readings to be read at certain times of the year is called a:
   a) lectionary
   b) liturgy
   c) vestment
   d) Eucharist
4 A set form of public worship is known as a:
   a) lectionary
   b) liturgy
   c) vestment
   d) Eucharist

Activities

Complete the answers to these questions:

1 Outline three types of Christian worship.

Christians worship in many ways. One type of worship is liturgical which follows a set pattern. Another type is ....

A third type is ....

2 Explain two reasons why Christians worship God in different ways. In your answer you must refer to a source of wisdom and authority.

The letter to the Hebrews tells Christians: ....

Some Christians find it easiest to carry this out through .... worship because .... Other Christians find it easiest to carry this out through .... worship because ....

Exam support

You might be asked to evaluate a statement such as:

God does not need people to worship him.

The table below might help you answer such a question.

Arguments for	Arguments against
God is an infinite being who cannot need the worship of finite beings.	God may not need people's worship but people need to worship him because doing so enables them to show their love of God.
God is perfect so he cannot need to be praised by people who are far from perfect.	Worship is a way for people to communicate with God and build a relationship with him.
God is omniscient so he knows what people need and want without them asking him.	Worship is a way for people to express their thanks and devotion to God.
God is all-good so he does not need people to tell him he is good.	Worship is part of the life of the Church and binds Christians into the Christian community.

Topic 1.3.2 The role of the sacraments in Christian life

REVISED

Sacraments are outward signs of an inward gift from God. There are seven sacraments in the Catholic and Orthodox Churches – baptism, reconciliation (penance), **Holy Communion** (Eucharist), confirmation, the anointing of the sick, holy orders and marriage.

The sacraments are essential in the life of Catholic, Orthodox and some Anglican Christians because through sacraments they receive grace from God, which makes their faith stronger.

Most Protestant, and many Anglican, Christians only have two sacraments – baptism and Holy Communion.

Some Christians, such as the Quakers and the Salvation Army, do not have any sacraments at all.

Baptism

All Christians who believe in sacraments in any way believe that Christians must be baptised, because baptism:

- is necessary for the person to receive salvation
- makes a person a member of the Church
- washes away original sin and makes the person pure
- allows them to receive the other sacraments.

Catholic Christians are usually baptised as babies (infant baptism). Parents and godparents bring the child to church and make promises to raise the child as a Catholic. The priest pours water over the child, baptising it in the name of the Trinity. He anoints the child with the oil of **chrism** and the godparents are given a lighted candle to hold.

Baptist Christians practise **believers' baptism** by **total immersion**. They believe that people need to make their own decision to become a member of Christ's Church. Baptist churches have a baptismal pool, where the minister baptises people in the name of the Trinity.

The Eucharist

The Eucharist began with the Last Supper Jesus had with his disciples.

The Eucharist in the Catholic Church is part of the service known as the Mass. Catholics are expected to attend Mass every Sunday. The Mass includes confession and **absolution**, prayers of intercession to help others, a special prayer changing the bread and wine into the body and blood of Christ **(transubstantiation)**, the people exchanging the peace and receiving the **consecrated hosts** and wine (drunk from a **chalice**). Any remaining consecrated hosts are placed in the tabernacle. The Mass is important to Catholics because they believe that during the Mass bread and wine are turned into the body and blood of Christ joining them with Jesus in the communion. Mass reminds Catholics that there is eternal life and assures them that they will inherit eternal life

In the Methodist Church, the Eucharist is known as Holy Communion and is usually celebrated once a month. Methodists believe Holy Communion is a remembrance and the bread and wine do not change, but it does bring unity and peace and closeness to Jesus. The bread is normal bread and the wine is non-alcoholic.

Absolution – the pardoning of sins through the actions and words of a priest or minister

Believers' baptism – baptism restricted to those old enough to understand the meaning of the ritual

Chalice – a large cup/goblet used for communion wine

Chrism – oil used for baptism and confirmation

Consecrated host – a communion wafer which has been blessed

Holy Communion – the Christian service of thanksgiving using bread and wine, also called the Eucharist or Mass

Total immersion – baptising by dipping the whole body under the water

Transubstantiation – the belief that during the service of Mass (also called Eucharist and Holy Communion) the bread and wine transform into the body and blood of Jesus

Sources of wisdom and authority

- The 39 Articles of the Church of England say that baptism and Eucharist are the only sacraments established by Jesus.
- The Catechism says that the sacraments, especially the Eucharist, bring communion with God and are essential for salvation.

Now test yourself

TESTED

1 Absolution is:
   a) a priest/minister forgiving a person's sins
   b) a priest/minister assuring someone that their sins have been forgiven
   c) the pardon of sins
   d) confession of sins
2 The chalice is:
   a) a communion wafer
   b) a large cup/goblet for communion wine
   c) oil used for baptism and confirmation
   d) a communion wafer which has been blessed
3 Chrism is:
   a) a communion wafer
   b) a large cup/goblet for communion wine
   c) oil used for baptism and confirmation
   d) a communion wafer which has been blessed
4 The consecrated host is:
   a) a communion wafer
   b) a large cup/goblet for communion wine
   c) oil used for baptism and confirmation
   d) a communion wafer which has been blessed

Activities

Complete the answers to these questions:

1 Outline three features of a Catholic Eucharist.

The main feature of a Catholic Eucharist is the prayer which changes the bread and wine into the body and blood of Jesus. Another feature is ....

A third feature is ....

2 Explain two reasons why baptism is important for most Christians. In your answer you must refer to a source of wisdom and authority.

Baptism is important for most Christians because they believe that being baptised is essential to be saved from sin and to become a member of the Church. According to the 39 Articles of the Church of England, baptism and the Eucharist are the only sacraments established by Jesus.

Baptism is also important because ....

Exam support

You might be asked to evaluate a statement such as:

You don't need to take the sacraments to be a good Christian.

The table below might help you answer such a question.

Arguments for	Arguments against
Quaker and Salvation Army Christians do not have any sacraments, but they are regarded as good Christians.	Without the sacrament of baptism, Christians cannot have their sins forgiven.
Jesus did not say that Christians have to take sacraments.	Without the sacrament of baptism, Christians cannot join the Church.
Jesus said that Christians need to love God and love their neighbour.	Through sacraments Christians receive grace from God, are made stronger in their faith and come closer to God.
In the Parable of the Sheep and the Goats, Jesus said that only those who helped the less fortunate would get into heaven, not those who take the sacraments.	Without the sacrament of the Eucharist, Christians cannot be united with Christ.

Topic 1.3.3 The nature and purpose of prayer

REVISED

The purpose of prayer

The main purpose of prayer is an attempt to contact God, usually through words. Prayer can have other purposes:

- **Adoration** – praising or adoring God for what he is, for example, 'O God, how great and marvellous you are'.
- **Thanksgiving** – thanking God either for his general goodness or for some specific thing.
- **Confession** – confessing sins to God, asking his forgiveness and determining to do better.
- **Supplication** – asking for God's help either for oneself or for others (also known as intercession).

Prayers can be expressed in different ways:

- **Vocal prayer** – when words are used, either out loud or mentally.
- **Meditation** – thinking about religious matters.
- **Contemplation** – communion with God.
- Set prayers – such as those used in liturgical worship, which many Christians come to know off by heart and use as their own prayers.

The Lord's Prayer

This is the main Christian prayer and Christians use it in both public and private prayer. It was taught by Jesus in the Gospels. The Lord's Prayer expresses:

- Adoration: '... hallowed be your name, your kingdom come, your will be done on earth as it is in heaven'.
- Confession: 'Forgive us our debts, as we also have forgiven our debtors'.
- Supplication: 'Give us today our daily bread ... And lead us not into temptation, but deliver us from the evil one'.

When each type of prayer is used

Set prayers are used in liturgical worship, but can also be used by Christians in their personal prayers when they wake up, when they go to bed and whenever they become aware of people suffering. Other Christians will use informal prayers on these occasions.

Why Christians pray

- Prayers of thanksgiving help Christians to realise they depend on others, and not take things for granted.
- Prayers of confession help Christians face up to and learn from their mistakes so that their life improves.
- Prayers of supplication can help Christians to feel they are doing something for those who suffer and can inspire them to do something practical to help the less fortunate.
- Contemplative and meditative prayers can bring inner peace.

Adoration – praising or adoring God for what he is

Confession – prayers saying sorry for sins and asking God's forgiveness

Contemplation – communion with God

Meditation – thinking about religious matters

Supplication – prayers asking for God's help

Thanksgiving – prayers thanking God

Vocal prayer – prayer using words

Sources of wisdom and authority

- Jesus said that Christians should not have long prayers because God knows what we want before we say anything.
- Jesus gave the Lord's Prayer in Matthew's Gospel as the best way to pray.
- St Paul said that Christians should pray at all times.

Now test yourself

TESTED

1 Prayers when people try to achieve communion with God are called:
   a) contemplation
   b) confession
   c) meditation
   d) supplication
2 Prayers saying sorry for sins and asking God's forgiveness are called:
   a) contemplation
   b) confession
   c) meditation
   d) supplication
3 Prayers asking for God's help are called:
   a) contemplation
   b) confession
   c) meditation
   d) supplication
4 Prayers when people simply think about religious matters are called:
   a) contemplation
   b) confession
   c) meditation
   d) supplication

Activities

Complete the answers to these questions:

1 Outline three purposes of prayer.

One purpose of prayer is adoration, praising God for what he is. Another purpose is ....

....

A third purpose is ....

2 Explain two reasons why the Lord's Prayer is important for Christians. In your answer you must refer to a source of wisdom and authority.

The Lord's Prayer is important for Christians because it is the prayer which Jesus taught Christians to use in the Gospels.

It is also important because it fulfils the main purposes of prayer, which are ....

....

Exam support

You might be asked to evaluate a statement such as:

Everyone needs to pray.

The table below might help you answer such a question.

Arguments for	Arguments against
St Paul says in Ephesians 6, 'And pray in the Spirit on all occasions with all kinds of prayers and requests'.	Atheists do not need to pray to God because they do not believe he exists.
Prayer is the way to contact God and as God is the creator and ruler of the universe, people need to contact him.	Jesus says in Matthew 6, 'your Father knows what you need before you ask him', so people cannot need to pray.
Everyone needs help from God and the way to gain God's help is to pray to him.	If God is omnibenevolent he will not punish people for not praying, so if people don't pray it won't matter.

Topic 1.3.4 Pilgrimage

REVISED

The nature, history and purpose of pilgrimage

Pilgrimage is a journey to a place of religious importance. Christians have been going on pilgrimage to the Holy Land since the Emperor Constantine's mother went there after she converted to Christianity. In the Middle Ages pilgrims spent years travelling to the Holy Land and visiting places connected with activities and/or **relics** of a saint to gain God's forgiveness for sins or healing from illness.

Pilgrimage became very popular with Catholics after St Bernadette of Lourdes saw the Virgin Mary and a miraculous spring appeared. Many healing miracles are alleged to have taken place there.

Christians go on pilgrimage:

- because Jesus went on pilgrimages to Jerusalem
- to become closer to God
- in the hope that some of the holiness of the saints will rub off on them
- to be cured from illness or gain inner strength to cope with illnesses.

Where do Christians go on pilgrimage?

There are four pilgrimage sites of special importance to Christians today:

- Jerusalem is the major centre of Christian pilgrimage, where the crucial events in the last week of Jesus' life took place. The most important sites are: the **Cenacle** where Jesus instituted the Eucharist at the Last Supper, the Via Dolorosa (the route Jesus took as he was made to carry his cross to Golgotha) and the Church of the Holy Sepulchre which contains the tomb where Jesus was buried and rose from the dead.
- Walsingham, (the English Nazareth), is a village in Norfolk, which had a copy of Mary's house in Nazareth built, based on a vision. It was rebuilt after the Reformation and pilgrims feel close to 'Our Lady of Walsingham' when they pray there. The shrine brings Catholics and Anglicans together, and healings have taken place there.
- Iona is a small island just off the west coast of Scotland where St Columba established a monastery to train missionaries to convert Scotland to Christianity. The monastery was rebuilt as a centre for all Christians, whatever their denomination. It now allows clergy and ordinary Christians from all denominations to spend time together and learn from each other.
- Taizé is an **ecumenical** monastery order in the south of France, founded to help bring together different Christians and different races to bring lasting peace to Europe after the Second World War. Young Christians go to Taizé each year for prayer, Bible study, sharing and communal work, giving them an opportunity to meet and learn from young people from different branches of Christianity and different races.

Most Protestant Christians feel that emphasising special 'holy places' is wrong because believers can encounter God anywhere. They oppose any form of worshipping the Virgin Mary and think that any **veneration** of saints and relics is wrong, because only God should be worshipped. So Protestants will visit the holy places in Jerusalem and go to Iona and Taizé, but will not go to Walsingham or places like Lourdes.

Cenacle – the Upper Room in Jerusalem where the Last Supper took place

Ecumenical – promoting Christian unity

Relic – the physical remains of a saint or the personal effects of a saint or holy person

Shrine – a place of worship that holds the tomb or relic of a saint

Veneration – treating with deep respect

Sources of wisdom and authority

- One of the Ten Commandments says that people should not bow down to or worship idols and images.
- Luke's Gospel records that Jesus went on pilgrimage to Jerusalem every Passover.

Now test yourself

TESTED

1 The Cenacle is:
   a) the Upper Room in Jerusalem where the Last Supper took place
   b) promoting Christian unity
   c) part of a dead saint's body or belongings
   d) to treat with deep religious respect
2 A relic is:
   a) the Upper Room in Jerusalem where the Last Supper took place
   b) promoting Christian unity
   c) part of a dead saint's body or belongings
   d) to treat with deep religious respect
3 Ecumenical is:
   a) the Upper Room in Jerusalem where the Last Supper took place
   b) promoting Christian unity
   c) part of a dead saint's body or belongings
   d) to treat with deep religious respect
4 Veneration is:
   a) the Upper Room in Jerusalem where the Last Supper took place
   b) promoting Christian unity
   c) part of a dead saint's body or belongings
   d) treating with deep religious respect

Activities

Complete the answers to these questions:

1 Outline three places of Christian pilgrimage.

Christians go on pilgrimage to Walsingham to the site where a replica of Mary's house was built. They also visit ....

A third place is ....

2 Explain two reasons why pilgrimage is important to many Christians. In your answer you must refer to a source of wisdom and authority.

One reason pilgrimage is important to many Christians is because pilgrims are following the example of Jesus. As Luke's Gospel records that ....

Another reason pilgrimage is important is ....

Exam support

You might be asked to evaluate a statement such as:

All Christians should go on pilgrimage to Jerusalem.

The table below might help you answer such a question.

Arguments for	Arguments against
Christians can visit the places where the crucial events in the last week of Jesus' life took place.	Many Christians have more important Christian duties to fulfil such as helping the less fortunate.
They can meditate in the Cenacle where Jesus instituted the Eucharist at the Last Supper.	Christians bringing up a family should put the needs of their family first.
They can walk along the Via Dolorosa which is the route Jesus took as he was made to carry his cross to Golgotha.	Pilgrimage is expensive and Christians should use their spare money to help the less fortunate, as shown by Jesus in the Parable of the Sheep and the Goats.
Christians can contemplate the resurrection in the Church of the Holy Sepulchre where Jesus was buried and rose from the dead.	All the things done on pilgrimage can be done by meditating on the accounts in the Bible and by watching a pilgrimage video.

Topic 1.3.5 Christian religious celebrations

REVISED

Christmas

Christians prepare for the coming of Jesus during the four weeks of **Advent**, when Christians remember the Old Testament prophecies about the coming of Jesus. Towards the end of Advent, Anglican and **Nonconformist** Christians have carol services such as the Festival of Lessons and Carols.

Christmas is celebrated with:

- services at midnight on Christmas Eve, when a crib is often set up and blessed
- services on the morning of Christmas Day which recall the Gospel accounts of Christmas
- a focus on the family life of Jesus on the Sunday after Christmas.

Christmas is significant for Christians because:

- Christmas is the celebration of the **Incarnation**, when Christians believe God became man as Jesus, and without the birth of Jesus Christ, there would be no Christianity
- celebrating the birth of Christ unites Christians and reminds them that all Christians, whatever their colour or ethnicity, share a common faith
- Christmas shows the importance of the family, because Jesus was born into a human family.

Advent – season before Christmas, remembering the first coming of Jesus and that he will come again

Incarnation – the belief that God took human form in Jesus

Nonconformist – a Protestant in England who is not a member of the Church of England

Salvation – the act of delivering from sin or saving from evil

Stations of the cross – fourteen pictures representing stages on Christ's way to crucifixion

Holy Week

Christians prepare for Easter in Holy Week by:

- processing near the church on Palm Sunday with palm leaves or branches, and distributing palm crosses
- a special Eucharist on Maundy Thursday when the priest or minister washes people's feet as Jesus washed the disciples' feet
- a walk of witness on Good Friday, followed by a three-hour afternoon service marking the time Jesus was on the cross. Catholic churches have prayers at the **stations of the cross**.

The significance of Holy Week

- Palm Sunday reminds Christians that Jesus is the Messiah, the Son of God who is worthy of their praise and adoration.
- Maundy Thursday reminds Christians of the origins and importance of the Eucharist.
- Holy Week reminds Christians of the **salvation** brought by Jesus and of the suffering he experienced, which will give them strength to cope with the suffering they may face.

Easter Day

- Some Christians (especially Catholics) celebrate with an Easter Vigil, which involves a ceremony of light to remember the darkness of the tomb and the joy and light of the resurrection. The Easter Vigil also includes a renewal of baptismal vows to remember the rebirth brought by Easter.
- All Christians have a joyful service to celebrate the resurrection of Jesus and the hope for eternal life which this brings to individual Christians.

Easter is an extremely significant event for Christians because it:

- celebrates the resurrection of Christ which Christians believe proves he is God's Son, as only God could rise from the dead
- assures the forgiveness of sins and people's restoration to God
- gives Christians the assurance that Jesus is alive to help and guide his Church.

Sources of wisdom and authority

- The Catechism says that the wonder of Christmas is that God became man.
- St Paul says in 1 Corinthians that Christ's resurrection guarantees life after death for Christ's faithful followers.
- St Paul says in 2 Corinthians that the essential Christian message is that Jesus died for our sins, was buried and rose on the third day.

Now test yourself

TESTED

1 Incarnation is:
   a) the season before Christmas, remembering the first coming of Jesus and that he will come again
   b) the belief that God took human form in Jesus
   c) a Protestant in England who is not a member of the Church of England
   d) the act of delivering from sin or saving from evil

2 Nonconformist is:
   a) the season before Christmas remembering the first coming of Jesus and that he will come again
   b) the belief that God took human form in Jesus
   c) a Protestant in England who is not a member of the Church of England
   d) the act of delivering from sin or saving from evil

3 Advent is:
   a) the season before Christmas, remembering the first coming of Jesus and that he will come again
   b) the belief that God took human form in Jesus
   c) a Protestant in England who is not a member of the Church of England
   d) the act of delivering from sin or saving from evil

4 Salvation is:
   a) the season before Christmas, remembering the first coming of Jesus and that he will come again
   b) the belief that God took human form in Jesus
   c) a Protestant in England who is not a member of the Church of England
   d) the act of delivering from sin or saving from evil

Activities

Complete the answers to these questions:

1 Outline three ways in which Christians celebrate Holy Week.

On Palm Sunday Christians process near the church and distribute palm crosses. On Maundy Thursday they ....

On Good Friday they ....

2 Explain two reasons why Christmas is significant for Christians. In your answer you must refer to a source of wisdom and authority.

Christmas is significant for Christians because it is the celebration of the Incarnation, when Christians believe God became man as Jesus. Without the birth of Jesus Christ, there would be no Christianity. As the Catechism of the Catholic Church says ....

Christmas is also significant because ....

Exam support

You might be asked to evaluate a statement such as:

Christmas is more important than Easter.

The table below might help you answer such a question.

Arguments for	Arguments against
Christmas is the celebration of the Incarnation and without the birth of Jesus Christ, there would be no Christianity.	Easter celebrates the resurrection of Christ, which Christians believe proves the identity of Jesus. If Jesus rose from the dead, he must have been both human and divine.
Celebrating Christmas unites Christians and reminds them that all Christians, whatever their colour or ethnicity, share a common faith.	Through the resurrection of Jesus, forgiveness of sins is assured and people can be restored to God.
Christmas shows the importance of the family as Jesus was born into a human family.	Easter assures Christians that Jesus is alive to help and guide his Church and to be with individual Christians.
Christmas is a time when Christians are asked to look at their lives and examine whether they are living in a holy way.	Easter proves that there is eternal life. Since Jesus rose from the dead, his faithful followers are assured that they too will have life after death with God in his Kingdom.

Topic 1.3.6 The future of the Church

REVISED

The purpose of missionary and evangelical work is to convert the world to Christianity. Christians are involved in this because it was the last command of Jesus to his disciples. Christians call this command to preach the gospel to the whole world the '**Great Commission**' and they believe it is something they must do.

The history of missionary and evangelical work

Jesus' disciples began missionary work immediately. St Peter organised missions throughout Palestine and is believed to have been the first Bishop of Rome. St Paul founded Christian churches throughout the Eastern Mediterranean and by 1000CE Christianity had spread throughout Europe and North Africa and had reached India and China.

The missionary work continued, with Christian churches established in Egypt, Iraq, North Africa, Iran, India and the European parts of the Roman Empire, including Britain by 100CE, China by 600CE and Russia by 900CE.

When Europeans began to **colonise** America and Africa, Christian missionaries went with them. South and Central America became Catholic through the work of Spanish and Portuguese missionaries; North America and much of Africa south of the Sahara became Protestant through the work of British missionaries.

Missionary and evangelical work is organised by Churcher Together and includes:

- The **Alpha** course, which aims to introduce non-churchgoers to the basics of the Christian faith and is run in UK churches by all the major Christian denominations.
- Hope, which provides resources and ideas for **evangelisation** in local communities.
- Scripture Union, which uses social media such as YouTube and Facebook to bring the Gospel to those outside the Church as well as working in schools, youth camps, etc.
- The 'Pontifical Council for the promotion of New Evangelisation', aims to renew the Catholic Church in the UK and is centred on local Catholic cathedrals.

Most conservative Catholic, and all Evangelical Christians, believe that missionary and evangelical work is very important because:

- the Great Commission of Jesus told Christians their duty was to preach the gospel to all nations and bring the world to the Christian faith
- they believe they should share their faith with others out of love for them because being a Christian helps people to share in God's love
- they believe that only by becoming a Christian can people outside the faith be assured a place in heaven.

Many Liberal Christians feel that missionary and evangelical work is no longer important because:

- the most important commandment of Jesus was to love God and love your neighbour, and they think it is difficult to love your neighbour if you are telling them their religion is wrong
- trying to convert others means you think your religion is right and theirs is wrong, but it is impossible to confirm this unless you have studied all the religions and proved them wrong
- there are many problems with overseas missionary work which can be seen as a new form of colonisation.

Alpha – the Christian course trying to convert non-churchgoers

Colonise – to take control of another race or culture

Evangelisation – seeking to convert to Christianity

Great Commission – Jesus' last command to his disciples to go out and convert the world

Sources of wisdom and authority

- Matthew's Gospel records that Jesus' last command was to tell his disciples to go and make disciples of all nations. This is known as the Great Commission.
- John's Gospel records that in his last words on earth, Jesus sent his disciples into the world, just as God had sent him.

Now test yourself

TESTED

1 The Alpha course:
   a) is run by the Catholic Church
   b) tries to bring Europeans back to the Church
   c) tries to convert non-churchgoers to Christianity
   d) is run by Churches Together
2 Colonisation is:
   a) a war of conquest
   b) one race or culture occupying another
   c) one religion converting another
   d) a course run by Churches Together
3 Evangelisation is:
   a) Protestants trying to convert Catholics
   b) one race or culture occupying another
   c) one religion trying to convert another
   d) seeking to convert to Christianity
4 The Great Commission is:
   a) Jesus' command to love God and love your neighbour
   b) Jesus' command to give to the poor
   c) Jesus' last command to his disciples to go out and convert the world
   d) Jesus' command to baptise in the name of the Father, the Son and the Holy Spirit

Activities

Complete the answers to these questions:

1 Outline three ways in which Christians carry out evangelical work in the UK.

Churches Together organises the Alpha Course, which aims to introduce non-churchgoers to the basics of the Christian faith. They also organise ....

Another way is ....

2 Explain two reasons why Christians carry out missionary work. In your answer you must refer to a source of wisdom and authority.

Christians carry out missionary work because Jesus told them to. His final words to his disciples in John were that he was sending ....

Jesus gave Christians a duty to convert the whole world, known as the Great Commission, when he told his disciples ....

Exam support

You might be asked to evaluate a statement such as:

All Christians should be missionaries.

The table below might help you answer such a question.

Arguments for	Arguments against
The Great Commission of Jesus told Christians their duty was to preach the gospel to all nations.	The most important commandment of Jesus was to love God and love your neighbour, and it is difficult to love your neighbour if you are telling them their religion is wrong.
Christians should share their faith with others out of love for them; being a Christian helps people to share in God's love.	Treating people differently because of their religion and trying to convert other religions is discrimination.
Only by becoming a Christian can people outside the faith be assured a place in heaven.	Trying to convert others means you think your religion is right and theirs is wrong, but you cannot say this unless you have studied all the religions and proved them wrong.

Topic 1.3.7 The importance of the local church

REVISED

A local Christian church is the centre of Christian identity and worship:

- It is where people go to show their devotion to God in Sunday services such as the Mass.
- Special services are held for Christians to celebrate Christian festivals.
- It offers the sacraments to the people – all churches provide baptism and Holy Communion, with Catholic and High Anglican churches also providing the other sacraments.
- It provides marriage services for couples wanting a church wedding.
- The local church provides worship and discussion groups, helping people to learn more about God and how Christians should behave.
- It enables people to share in worship with Christians in their local area, giving a sense of belonging and strengthening the community.

Local churches help the local area by:

- supporting local Christian schools (most areas have both Catholic and Church of England primary and secondary schools)
- providing social facilities such as youth clubs, uniformed organisations and toddler groups, so helping fulfil people's need to socialise and make friends
- supporting and putting people in contact with Christians that provide support and advice for families that are experiencing difficulties
- providing financial support if, for example, the family wage earner is ill or made redundant
- providing legal advice clinics to help people cope with legal problems
- supporting causes such as Church Action on Poverty, which works with local churches and with people in poverty themselves to find solutions
- providing help for the needy through running **food banks** and helping with local hostels for the homeless, etc.

By these means the Church shows love for those in need, as requested by Jesus in the Parable of the Sheep and the Goats.

Prayer groups – groups of Christians who join together to pray and increase their understanding of prayer

Ecumenism – movement working for co-operation between the Churches and eventual Church unity

Food bank – a charitable organisation that distributes food to people who have insufficient money for food

Sermons – talks on a religious subject (usually based on a Bible passage)

The local church and ecumenism

Local churches are usually part of a local Churches Together group where they:

- commit to work together – this is known as **ecumenism**
- have joint activities such as services, social gatherings and discussion groups
- work together for Christian charities
- work together to help people in the local area know about the Christian churches in the area and what facilities they provide
- In places where there is only one church building they involve all who wish to worship locally in a shared use of the premises for worship.

A local church provides an individual believer with an opportunity:

- to worship
- to partake in the sacraments
- to deepen their faith through **sermons**, discussion, **prayer groups** and Bible study groups, etc.
- for Christian fellowship with other Christians.

The church does this because it believes it is part of the Body of Christ and that it must welcome, nurture and provide spiritual sustenance for fellow members of Christ's body.

Sources of wisdom and authority

- St Peter told Church leaders to be shepherds of God's flock.
- The Catechism says that it is the task of the local parish to bring people into the life of the Church and help the local area through good works and brotherly love.

Now test yourself

TESTED

1 A group of Christians who join together learn from each other about issues facing Christians is called:
   a) A sermon
   b) A discussion group
   c) An Alpha group
   d) A support group

2 Working for cooperation between the Churches and eventual Church unity is called:
   a) Evangelism
   b) Charity
   c) Ecumenism
   d) Fundamentalism

3 A charitable organisation that distributes food to people having insufficient money for food is called a:
   a) Aid Bank
   b) Help Bank
   c) Food Bank
   d) Charity Bank

4 A talk on a religious subject (usually based on a Bible passage) is called a:
   a) Liturgy
   b) Sacrament
   c) Sermon
   d) Catechism

Activities

Complete the answers to these questions:

1 Outline three ways in which the local church is important for the local Christian community.

The local church is important because it provides Sunday services so that people can show their devotion to God.

It also ....

A third way is ....

2 Explain two reasons why the local church is important for the local area. In your answer you must refer to a source of wisdom and authority.

The local church is important for the local area because it provides facilities that might not otherwise be provided. For example, causes such as Church Action on Poverty work with local churches and with people in poverty themselves to find solutions to poverty. The local church does this because St Peter told local Church leaders to be shepherds of God's flock.

It is also important because ....

Exam support

You might be asked to evaluate a statement such as:

Each area should just have one Christian church – it's not necessary to have separate churches for each denomination.

The table below might help you answer such a question.

Arguments for	Arguments against
Christians are supposed to be the Body of Christ on earth and so they should be united by worshipping in one church.	There need to be separate churches so that there can be different types of worship (such as liturgical and non-liturgical).
Maintaining one church is less expensive and would leave extra money to be spent on the poor.	Different denominations have different types of ministries – Pentecostals might find it difficult being led by a Catholic priest and vice versa.
One church would make it easier and more effective to organise local Christians to serve the local community.	Denominations have different interpretations of Christianity which might lead to debate and division rather than concentrating on Christian mission.
Christians are committed to Churches Together and if there were only one local church all Christians would be together.	Having one church for an area could lead to division as an area would have to choose which churches to close and which to keep.

Topic 1.3.8 The worldwide Church

REVISED

The Church in the world

Christianity is the world's largest religion, a third of the world's population is Christian (2.4 billion Christians).

The Church and reconciliation

Pope Francis and other Church leaders continually work for peace and **reconciliation** by trying to bring people in conflict together because:

- the forgiveness of sins brought by the death of God's son, Jesus, has allowed reconciliation between God and humans
- Jesus said that if people do not forgive those who have sinned against them, God will not forgive their sins
- St Paul said that Christians should try to live in peace with everyone.

Problems faced by the persecuted Church

There are a few countries in the world where it is not safe to be a Christian. In dictatorships like North Korea, Christians must worship secretly and thousands of Christians have been imprisoned. In Muslim countries that operate a strict form of **Shari'ah law**, it is difficult to be a Christian and impossible to try to convert others, since converting to another religion is a criminal offence. In areas of Iraq taken over by Islamic State (Isis), most churches have been demolished and many Christians have been killed.

Christian teachings about charity

Christianity teaches that Christians should share the good things of the earth to help others:

- Jesus said that the greatest commandments are to love God and love your neighbour.
- In 1 Corinthians 13, St Paul teaches that love is greater than any other spiritual gift. He says that it does not matter how many religious things you do; without love, none of these things matter.
- In the Parable of the Sheep and the Goats, Jesus says that he will judge people at the end of the world and separate people like a shepherd separates sheep from goats. The sheep are those who helped Jesus when he needed it and they will go to heaven because whatever they did for someone suffering like this, they did for Jesus. However, the goats will go to hell because they did not do any of these things for other people and so they did not do them for Jesus.

Christian Aid

Christian Aid campaigns to end world poverty by:

- campaigning to cancel the debt owed by some of the world's poorest countries
- educating people in the UK on the need for and benefits of helping countries in the developing world
- promoting **Fairtrade** to ensure better prices, improved working conditions, local sustainability and fair terms of trade for farmers and workers
- helping in times of natural disaster and providing aid to refugees by sending water and food, antibiotics and shelters.

Christian Aid is trying to end world poverty because of Christian teachings about charity.

Fairtrade – a group aiming to help producers in developing countries achieve better trading conditions

Reconciliation – bringing together people who were opposed to each other

Shari'ah law – Islamic law based on the Qur'an and the sayings of Muhammad

Steward – someone appointed to look after something on behalf of someone else

Sources of wisdom and authority

- Jesus said 'Whatever you did for one of the least of these brothers of mine, you did for me'.
- The House of Bishops of the Church of England issued a statement that Christians are called to help the poor.
- St Paul says in 1 Corinthians, 'And now these three remain: faith, hope and love. But the greatest of these is love'.

Now test yourself

TESTED

1 In which of these countries are Christians more likely to face persecution?
a) India
b) South Korea
c) Sudan
d) Japan

2 Who said, 'But the greatest of these is love'?
a) St Matthew
b) St Paul
c) St Luke
d) St John

3 Which of the following tries to improve trading conditions for producers in developing countries?
a) Fair markets
b) Fairtrade
c) Fair banks
d) Fair interest

4 Someone appointed to look after something on behalf of someone else is a:
a) manager
b) Caliph
c) steward
d) substitute

Activities

Complete the answers to these questions:

1 Outline three activities of Christian Aid aimed at improving life in developing countries.

Christian Aid runs development projects such as helping small groups set up businesses.

It also organises ....

Another activity of Christian Aid is ....

2 Explain two reasons why Christians work to end world poverty. In your answer you must refer to a source of wisdom and authority.

Christians work to end world poverty because St Paul taught about the importance of love in 1 Corinthians and because of statements by the House of Bishops of the Church of England that said Christians have a duty to help the poor.

They also work to end world poverty because of the parable Jesus told about ....

....

Exam support

You might be asked to evaluate a statement such as: *It is easy to be a Christian in the world today.*

The table below might help you answer such a question.

Arguments for	Arguments against
There are Christians all over the world.	There are places in the world (e.g. North Korea and some Muslim countries) where Christians are not allowed to practise their faith.
In most countries there are no laws making it difficult to be a Christian.	Most people in the UK are not religious and they can make being a Christian appear uncool.
Christians need to love God and there are lots of churches around the world where God can be worshipped.	It can be very difficult to find the time to pray and worship God properly.
Christians need to love their neighbour and there are lots of charities like Christian Aid which Christians can support.	Following Jesus' commands about loving your neighbour can be very difficult – there are so many people in need that it's difficult to know where to stop and how much of your income you should spend on yourself.

1.4 Matters of life and death

Topic 1.4.1 Origins and value of the universe

REVISED

The Big Bang theory says that matter is eternal, and about 13.7 billion years ago, the matter became so compressed that it produced an explosion called the Big Bang. As the matter of the universe flew away from the explosion, the forces of gravity joined some of the matter into stars and, about 5 billion years ago, our solar system was formed, evidenced by the Red-shift effect. Many Christians simply ignore the scientific **cosmology**, but others have responded in three ways:

- **Creationism** says that science is wrong and that all the evidence for the Big Bang can be explained by the effects of Noah's flood and the **Apparent Age** theory, which claims the universe is younger than it looks because although the earth was only six days old when Adam was born, it would have looked billions of years old. They believe God created the universe in the way described in the Bible (known as creationism).
- The intelligent design argument states that the universe depends on so many interacting parts and has such complex evidence of design that there must have been an intelligent designer – God – to set up the universe. They believe this means that neither Big Bang nor evolution could have happened by chance.
- The compatibility response claims that both the Big Bang and God are compatible because: the Big Bang had to be at exactly the right microsecond (too soon and it would have been too small to form stars, too late and everything would have gone too fast for stars to form); without scientific laws such as gravity the matter of the universe could not have formed solar systems and only God could have ensured these things happened.

The Big Bang was first proposed by Georges Lemaître, a Catholic priest and professor of physics, who said:

- the beginning of the universe was the beginning of time
- his theory neither proved nor disproved religion
- science and religion are separate fields of human experience which do not conflict with each other.

The value of the universe in Christian teaching

Christianity teaches that God created the universe and everything in it, and that he made it in such a way that it has produced an environment on earth which is perfectly suited for human life. God made everything in the way he intended it to be, and, 'God saw all that he had made and it was very good' (Genesis 1:31). So the universe has great value for Christians.

Some people think that the universe is a **commodity** to be used, or misused, as people wish. However, Christianity teaches that:

- the environment is a gift from God to humans and so must be treated with care
- humans have a responsibility to treat animals humanely and to treat the land kindly
- the Parable of the Talents means Christians have a responsibility to leave the earth a better place than they found it
- there will be a judgement day at the end of the world when people will be judged on how they have fulfilled their duty to preserve God's earth.

Apparent Age – the idea that the world would have looked billions of years old when it was only a second old

Commodity – something that humans need or want

Cosmology – a study/ explanation of the origins of the universe

Creationism – belief that the universe, and humans, were created in the way the Bible says

Sources of wisdom and authority

- Genesis says that when God saw all that he had made, he said it was very good.
- Genesis says that God allowed humans to rule over the fish of the sea, the birds of the air and animals.
- Pope Francis has said that the Big Bang does not contradict the intervention of God, but actually requires it.

Now test yourself

TESTED

1 What is a commodity?
   a) The idea that the world would have looked billions of years old when it was only a second old
   b) Something that humans need or want
   c) A study or explanation of the origins of the universe
   d) Belief that the universe, and humans, were created in the way the Bible says

2 What is cosmology?
   a) The idea that the world would have looked billions of years old when it was only a second old
   b) Something that humans need or want
   c) A study or explanation of the origins of the universe
   d) Belief that the universe, and humans, were created in the way the Bible says

3 What is Apparent Age?
   a) The idea that the world would have looked billions of years old when it was only a second old
   b) Something that humans need or want
   c) A study or explanation of the origins of the universe
   d) Belief that the universe, and humans, were created in the way the Bible says

4 What is creationism?
   a) The idea that the world would have looked billions of years old when it was only a second old
   b) Something that humans need or want
   c) A study or explanation of the origins of the universe
   d) Belief that the universe, and humans, were created in the way the Bible says

Activities

Complete the answers to these questions:

1 Outline three features of the work of Georges Lemaître.

Georges Lemaître was the first scientist to propose the Big Bang. He said ....

He also ....

2 Explain two reasons why Christians should not use the world as a commodity. In your answer you must refer to a source of wisdom and authority.

Christians believe that God created the environment as something which is good, so they have a duty to ensure that it continues to be what God intended, rather than treating God's world as a commodity. Genesis says that God saw what he had made and said it was very good.

Another reason Christians should not treat the world as a commodity is because ....

Exam support

You might be asked to evaluate a statement such as:

God created the world.

The table below might help you answer such a question.

Arguments for	Arguments against
It is what the Bible says.	The evidence of science is that the matter of the universe is eternal and so was never created.
The universe depends on so many interacting parts that it could not have happened by chance, only God could have done it.	The universe began with the Big Bang and the Red-shift effect shows the universe is still expanding from the initial point of the Big Bang.
The universe has so much complex evidence of design (e.g. DNA) that there must have been an intelligent designer – God – to set up the universe.	Background radiation throughout the universe has been discovered by radio telescopes and is thought to be a remnant of the Big Bang.
The Big Bang had to occur at exactly the right microsecond and only God could have done that.	Ripples detected by scientists in deep space are gravitational waves, which seem to have been triggered by the rapid expansion of the universe, during the Big Bang.

Topic 1.4.2 The sanctity of life

REVISED

Sanctity of life means that life is holy or sacred. Christians believe that human life is holy because it is a gift from God.

The Bible teaches that human life is precious and special in the following ways:

- Only humans have a soul because only humans were made in God's likeness.
- Human life is special because it comes directly from God.
- This special nature of human life is also shown in God's covenant with Noah after the flood, when God said that no one should kill because humans are made in God's image.
- The special nature of human life is shown in the Ten Commandments which say: 'You shall not murder'.
- St Paul said that life is sacred because the body is a temple of the Holy Spirit and so life is sacred because God's Spirit is in humans.

As well as for abortion and euthanasia (see pages 64 and 70), sanctity of life is important for Christian attitudes in a number of areas.

- **Killing in self-defence:** If human life is sacred, are Christians allowed to kill in self-defence? Most Christians would say that the sanctity of one's own life takes precedence over the sanctity of other people's lives. The Catholic Catechism says that killing in self-defence is not murder.
- **Killing in war:** Some Christians believe that the sanctity of life means they should never fight in wars. There are many Christian **pacifist** groups who base their pacifism on Jesus' command in the Sermon on the Mount to love your enemies. However, most Christians believe that they can fight in Just Wars because, as the Catholic Catechism says, the need to protect the innocent from aggressors justifies breaking the sanctity of life beliefs.
- **Capital punishment** Many Christians believe they should never use **capital punishment** because if life is sacred, capital punishment must be wrong. Other Christians believe that capital punishment can be used because the Bible gives the **death penalty** as the punishment for various offences, and the traditional teaching of the Churches allow it.

Although non-religious people do not believe that life has been created by God, most non-religious people (especially Humanists) believe that human life is precious and should be preserved. They base their ideas about sanctity of life on the UN Declaration of Human Rights Article 3, so they believe that:

- everyone has the right to life, so taking someone's life must be wrong
- killing in self-defence is acceptable if it is the only way to protect your own life
- fighting wars in self-defence is acceptable because it preserves other people's lives
- the death penalty is wrong because no court system can be sure that the correct verdict is always given. Wrongly convicted people can be released from prison, but not if they have been executed.

Capital punishment – the death penalty for a crime

Death penalty – execution ordered by a court of law

Pacifism – refusing to fight in wars

Sanctity of life – the belief that life is holy and is a gift from God

Sources of wisdom and authority

- The Catholic Catechism says that human life is sacred because it is created by God and God alone is the Lord of life.
- Genesis says that life is sacred because God made humans in his image.
- In his covenant with Noah after the flood, God said that no one should kill because humans are made in God's image.

Now test yourself

TESTED

1 The death penalty for a crime is called:
   a) sanctity of life
   b) legitimate
   c) pacifism
   d) capital punishment
2 If something is lawful it is called:
   a) sanctity of life
   b) legitimate
   c) pacifism
   d) capital punishment
3 Refusing to fight in wars is called:
   a) sanctity of life
   b) legitimate
   c) pacifism
   d) capital punishment
4 The belief that life is holy and belongs to God is called:
   a) sanctity of life
   b) legitimate
   c) pacifism
   d) capital punishment

Activities

Complete the answers to these questions:

1 Outline three issues where belief in the sanctity of life causes problems for Christians.

One issue is abortion and the sanctity of life of the foetus. Another issue is ....

....

A third issue is ....

2 Explain two reasons why Christians believe in the sanctity of life. In your answer you must refer to a source of wisdom and authority.

Christians believe in the sanctity of life because they believe that life is a gift from God. Because life is created by God, it should never be taken by humans. As God declared to Noah after the flood, ...

....

Another reason is ....

Exam support

You might be asked to evaluate a statement such as:

Christians should never take life.

The table below might help you answer such a question.

Arguments for	Arguments against
Life is created by God and belongs to its creator, so life and death decisions must be in the hands of God.	Christians believe in loving their neighbour which may justify taking the life of a foetus to preserve the life of the mother.
God created humans in his own image so there is a part of God in every human.	Christians believe it is right to take life if it is the only way of defending your own life.
God sanctified human life by becoming human. Jesus suffered without trying to shorten his sufferings which shows that life can only be ended when God decides.	Some Christians believe it is right to use capital punishment for some crimes.
Christians believe human bodies are the temple of the Holy Spirit and so are sacred.	Some Christians think it is right to fight in wars in order to protect the lives of other people.

Topic 1.4.3 The origins and value of human life

REVISED

The scientific explanation of the origin of human life is based on Darwin's theory of evolution. It states that:

- after the earth formed about 4.5 billion years ago, the combination of gases on the earth's surface produced primitive life forms
- the genetic structure of the offspring had slight differences from their parents (mutation)
- those offspring with changes better suited to living in their particular environment were more likely to survive (known as 'survival of the fittest)
- over millions of years this process led to vegetation, then invertebrate animals, then vertebrates and finally, about 2.5 million years ago, humans.

This process was called **natural selection** by Darwin and means that all species have developed naturally without divine intervention. The evidence for evolution is found in:

- The fossil record discovered by palaeontologists
- Genetics showing clear connections between dinosaurs and crocodiles
- Geneticists discovering that 50% of human DNA is the same as cabbages, showing a connection between animal and vegetable life.

Why evolution might cause issues for Christians

- Evolution challenges the authority of the Bible, because if evolution is correct then the Genesis creation stories are wrong.
- If humans have not been created by God, the purpose of life must be up to humans, not God. It is up to humans to decide what constitutes the value of human life, as human life cannot have sanctity since the sanctity of life depends on it being created by God.
- If evolution is true, there was no **Fall of Man** and no **original sin** and so there is no need for salvation and to atone for the death of Jesus.
- The Christian belief that humans have a soul because they were made in the image of God is impossible if they came from natural selection.

How Christians respond to evolution

Creationist Christians simply reject evolution. They believe that fossils are the remains of animal life that was destroyed by Noah's flood.

Some Christians believe that life is too complex to have evolved naturally and that the emergence of humans must have required divine help.

Many Christians believe that the way God made the universe was bound to result in evolution and the development of creatures like humans because of the laws of science and natural selection.

Special Agenda IV

A Church of England report urging the Church to show people that:

- science and religion go hand in hand rather than being opposed to each other
- science shows 'the amazing world God has created and the beauty and glory of God himself'
- science and religion working together can help humanity understand more about the world
- the Church helps and supports Christians working in science.

Fall of Man – the idea that when Adam disobeyed God by eating the forbidden fruit, sin came into the world

Fossil record – the evidence provided in fossils for evolution

Geneticists – scientists in the study of heredity and genes

Natural selection – the idea that life evolved through mutations, meaning those life forms better suited to the environment survived, and the less well suited died out

Original sin – the sin of Adam and Eve disobeying God, which some Christians believe is passed on to all humans at birth

Palaeontologists – scientists who study fossils

Sources of wisdom and authority

- Some Church leaders have said that evolution as an unguided, unplanned process cannot be true.
- Pope Francis has claimed that God created human beings and then let them develop according to the internal laws that he gave them.

Now test yourself

TESTED

1 The idea that when Adam disobeyed God by eating the forbidden fruit, sin came into the world, is known as:
   a) palaeontologists
   b) geneticists
   c) the Fall of Man
   d) natural selection

2 Experts in the study of heredity and genes are known as:
   a) palaeontologists
   b) geneticists
   c) the Fall of Man
   d) natural selection

3 The idea that life evolved through mutations better fitted to the environment surviving and the less fit dying out, is known as:
   a) palaeontologists
   b) geneticists
   c) the Fall of Man
   d) natural selection

4 Scientists who study fossils are known as:
   a) palaeontologists
   b) geneticists
   c) the Fall of Man
   d) natural selection

Activities

Complete the answers to these questions:

1 Outline three features of the non-religious explanation about the origins and value of human life.

One feature is that the combination of gases on the earth's surface produced single-celled life forms. Another feature is ....

A third feature is ....

2 Explain two reasons why evolution raises issues for Christians. In your answer you must refer to a source of wisdom and authority.

Christians believe that the world needed saving from the sin brought into the world by Adam, as claimed by St Paul and Jesus. However, evolution means that there was no Adam and no original sin and so no need for God to send his Son into the world.

Another issue raised by evolution is ....

Exam support

You might be asked to evaluate a statement such as: *Humans have been created by God.*

The table below might help you answer such a question.

Arguments for	Arguments against
It is what the Bible teaches in both the Old and New Testaments.	Palaeontologists have discovered that the older a fossil, the more simple its structure is, which must mean that species, including humans, have evolved through natural selection.
Humans are so different and complex that their emergence must have required the help of an intelligent designer such as God.	There are fossils of species that have become extinct (dinosaurs) and natural selection explains why a branch no longer suited to the environment will die out.
Only if humans have been created by God does life have meaning and purpose.	Genetics shows clear connections between dinosaurs and crocodiles and birds.
Evolution might explain developments within species, but only God and Genesis can explain the creation of species, especially a species like humans.	Geneticists have discovered that about 50 per cent of human DNA is the same as that of a cabbage, indicating an ancestral connection between animal and vegetable life.

Topic 1.4.4 The issue of abortion

REVISED

Abortion (termination) is the medical process of ending a pregnancy so it does not result in the birth of a baby.

British law on abortion is governed by the 1967 Abortion Act, which says abortion can only be carried out if two doctors agree that the mother's life is at risk, the mother's physical or mental health is at risk, the mental or physical health of existing children would be at risk or the baby might be born seriously disabled.

Christian attitudes to abortion

The Catholic and Evangelical Protestant Churches are **pro-life** and teach that abortion is wrong whatever the circumstances because:

- life is holy and belongs to God
- life begins at **conception** so abortion is taking life and the Ten Commandments teach that it is wrong to take life
- every person has a natural 'right to life'. A foetus is a human being and abortion destroys its right to life

Liberal Protestants are **pro-choice** and believe that although abortion is wrong, it must be permitted in certain circumstances because:

- Jesus told Christians to love their neighbour as themselves, and abortion may be the most loving thing to do
- life does not begin until a foetus is capable of surviving outside the mother's body
- the sanctity of life can be broken in such things as a Just War, so why not in a just abortion (e.g. when the mother's life is at risk)?

Atheist and Humanist attitudes to abortion

Most atheists and Humanists agree with abortion because they believe that:

- a foetus cannot be considered as a separate life until it is capable of living outside the mother
- a woman should have the right to do what she wants with her own body, some believe in abortion on demand
- abortion should be an automatic right for women who have been raped or subjected to incest or paedophilia.

Situation Ethics and abortion

Liberal Christians, Humanists and atheists often use Situation Ethics when considering an ethical problem. They look at the good and bad points of the possible choices and then determine what would be the most loving thing to do. So they would look at why a woman wants an abortion: if she had been raped, if having a baby would have a bad effect on her physical or mental health, or if the effect of another child on the rest of the family would be negative. They would then decide if an abortion would be the most loving thing in that situation.

Sources of wisdom and authority

- The Catechism says that human life must be respected and protected from the moment of conception, so abortion is wrong.
- The Methodist Church says that abortion is wrong, but must be allowed in many circumstances as it is the lesser of two evils.
- The Humanist and Ethical Union says abortion should be allowed because every child should be a wanted child.

Now test yourself

TESTED

1 The right to have an abortion whatever the woman's reasons is called:
   a) pro-choice
   b) abortion on demand
   c) pro-life
   d) conception
2 The name given to those who support a woman's right to abortion is:
   a) pro-choice
   b) abortion on demand
   c) pro-life
   d) conception
3 The fertilisation of the egg by the sperm is known as:
   a) pro-choice
   b) abortion on demand
   c) pro-life
   d) conception
4 The name given to those who think abortion should be banned is:
   a) pro-choice
   b) abortion on demand
   c) pro-life
   d) conception

Activities

Complete the answers to these questions:

1 Outline three requirements for an abortion to be legal in Great Britain.

Two doctors must agree that the mother's condition meets the requirements of the law. Another requirement is ....

A third requirement is ....

2 Explain two reasons why Catholics are against abortion. In your answer you must refer to a source of wisdom and authority.

One reason is that the Church teaches abortion is wrong because it says life begins at conception and so abortion is taking life. As Pope Paul VI said in Humanae Vitae, human life must be respected and protected from the moment of conception.

Another reason Catholics oppose abortion is ....

Exam support

You might be asked to evaluate a statement such as:

No Christian should ever have an abortion.

The table below might help you answer such a question.

Arguments for	Arguments against
Life is holy and belongs to God, therefore only God has the right to end a pregnancy.	Jesus told Christians to love their neighbour as themselves, and abortion may be the most loving thing to do in a woman's particular circumstances.
Life begins at conception so abortion is taking life; the Ten Commandments teach that it is wrong to take life.	Life does not begin until a foetus is capable of surviving outside the mother's body.
Every person has a natural 'right to life'. A foetus is a human being and abortion destroys its right to life.	Christianity is concerned with justice and if abortions were banned, an unjust situation would arise: rich women would pay for abortions in another country, but the poor would use 'back-street' abortionists.

Topic 1.4.5 Death and the afterlife

REVISED

All Christians believe in life after death for the following reasons:

- Jesus rose from the dead. All four Gospels record that Jesus was crucified and buried in a stone tomb and that, on the Sunday morning, some of his women disciples went to the tomb and found it empty. Different Gospels then record different 'resurrection appearances' of Jesus. The rest of the New Testament is full of references to the resurrection of Jesus. Clearly, if Jesus rose from the dead, then there is life after death.
- St Paul teaches in Corinthians and Ephesians that people will have a resurrection like that of Jesus.
- Jesus taught that he would come again at the end of the world for a final judgement resulting in heaven or hell.
- The major creeds of the Church teach that Jesus rose from the dead and that there will be life after death for Christians. Christians believe the creeds and so they believe in life after death.
- Many Christians believe that people are made up of a body and a soul (mind or personality). They believe that the soul is non-material and will never die. They believe that when the body dies, the soul leaves the body to live with God (**immortality of the soul**).

Immortality of the soul – the idea that the soul lives on after the death of the body

Mediums – people who claim to be able to communicate with the spirit world

Paranormal – unexplained events that are thought to have spiritual causes, for example, ghosts, mediums

Reincarnation – the belief that, after death, souls are reborn in a new body

Remembered lives – memories of a previous existence

Non-religious arguments for life after death

- The **paranormal** – such things as: near-death experiences when people are clinically dead for a period of time and then come back to life; evidence for a spirit world such as mediums contacting the dead in a spirit world
- **Remembered lives (reincarnation)** – some people claim to be able to remember themselves in other lives, such as **mediums** and clearly if people are reincarnated, there is life after death.
- **Comfort** – when someone dies it is almost impossible to believe that they are gone forever. Belief in an after-life gives the hope of meeting loved ones who have passed on
- **Logic** – the idea of an after-life where the evil are punished and the good rewarded makes sense of people's belief in justice and fair play.

Sources of wisdom and authority

- All four Gospels record that Jesus' body rose from the dead.
- St Paul says in 1 Corinthians that Jesus' resurrection is proof that Christians will have life after death.

Now test yourself

TESTED

1 The idea that the soul lives on after the death of the body is called:
a) infinity of the soul
b) immortality of the soul
c) inspiration of the soul
d) immanence of the soul

2 People who claim to be able to communicate with the spirit world are called:
a) medians
b) mediators
c) mediums
d) meditators

3 Unexplained things which are thought to have spiritual causes are called:
a) resurrection
b) reincarnation
c) paranormal
d) resuscitation

4 The belief that, after death, souls are reborn in a new body, is called:
a) resurrection
b) reincarnation
c) paranormal
d) resuscitation

Activities

Complete the answers to these questions:

1 Outline three different non-religious reasons for believing in life after death.

The paranormal, such as near-death experiences where people get a glimpse of an afterlife, is a Christian reason for believing in life after death. Another reason is remembered lives such a reincarnation. A third reason is ....

2 Explain two reasons why Christians believe in life after death. In your answer you must refer to a source of wisdom and authority.

The main reason Christians believe in life after death is because they believe that Jesus rose from the dead, and if Jesus rose from the dead there must be life after death. This is something that is recorded in all four of the Gospels and is referred to throughout the New Testament.

Another reason is ....

Exam support

You might be asked to evaluate a statement such as: *Only Christians have evidence for life after death.*

The table below might help you answer such a question.

Arguments for	Arguments against
The only clear evidence of someone coming back to life is the resurrection of Jesus, the founder of Christianity.	Near-death experiences are evidence for heaven and a life after death.
Plenty of Christians gave evidence of seeing the risen Jesus – 'he appeared to Cephas, and then to the Twelve. After that, he appeared to more than five hundred of the brothers and sisters at the same time.' (1 Corinthians 15:6)	Mediums who claim to communicate with the spirit world inhabited by those who have died are evidence of life after death.
The Christian holy book, the Bible, is believed to be God's word and gives plenty of evidence for life after death.	Many non-religious people claim to be able to remember themselves in other lives, so if people are reincarnated, there is life after death.
Christians claim to have had contact with the Virgin Mary and the saints, which is evidence of life after death.	We make sense of this life if we believe that after our deaths, those that are good will be rewarded while those who are evil will be punished.

Topic 1.4.6 Non-religious arguments against life after death

REVISED

Humanists and atheists reject the religious arguments for life after death because:

- Different religions have different ideas about life after death, whereas, if the idea were true, they would all say the same things about it.
- The religious evidence for life after death is based on holy books, but it is impossible for a non-believer to decide which religion's holy book comes from God.
- They think that the resurrection of Jesus is not based on sufficiently reliable evidence to prove the existence of an afterlife because the Bible accounts contain so many contradictions. For example, John's **Gospel** says Jesus' body was anointed with spices before being placed in the tomb, whereas the other three Gospels say that women brought spices to the tomb on Sunday morning to anoint Jesus' body.
- Evidence for near-death experiences is unreliable because much scientific work has shown that people have **fallible memories**.
- They think the evidence of mediums and reincarnation is suspect because much of it can be explained in other ways.

People also have their own reasons for believing there can be no life after death:

- Life after death depends on there being a God and they do not believe in God.
- Most beliefs in life after death assume that the mind or soul can survive in a **non-material** state without the body, but the evidence of science is that the human mind is totally dependent on the physical brain.
- They believe there is a problem as to where life after death could take place. Space exploration has shown there is no heaven above the sky and physics has shown there is no non-material world on earth.
- If there is a non-material afterlife, how would we recognise souls without bodies? If souls survive death, then they would be alone with no way of contacting other souls.
- Many agree with Karl Marx that belief in life after death was an invention of the ruling classes to be used to keep the working class happy with low wages and poor living conditions (**social control**) by promising them a reward in heaven – 'pie in the sky when you die'.

Christian responses to the non-religious arguments

Christianity reject these non-religious arguments because they believe:

- Christianity is the one true religion so the Bible and what it says can be relied on. This means other religions and holy books saying different things about life after death doesn't matter because the Bible record of the resurrection can be relied on.
- The disciples must have known whether or not the resurrection happened and they would not have risked their lives as they did for something they knew was a lie.
- The arguments of philosophers like René Descartes show that the mind is separate from the body and so could survive without the body.
- Heaven is a spiritual dimension, outside but interacting with the material universe.
- Belief in life after death might be a comfort when someone dies, but that is not proof it exists.

Fallible memories – memories that can be mistaken

Gospels – the books of Matthew, Mark, Luke and John which are the only record of Jesus' life

Non-material – not physical

Social control – regulating people's behaviour so that they conform to the rules of society

Sources of wisdom and authority

- St Paul says in 2 Timothy that all scripture is inspired by God.
- The Catechism says that God inspired the authors of the books of the Bible.

Now test yourself

TESTED

1 Regulating people's behaviour so that they conform with the rules of a society is known as:
   a) non-material
   b) Marxism
   c) sociology
   d) social control

2 One reason atheists reject belief in life after death is because:
   a) some religions do not say the same things about life after death
   b) different religions have different ideas about life after death
   c) different religions say the same thing about life after death
   d) some religions say the same thing about life after death

3 Christians believe the Bible gives reliable evidence because:
   a) they believe its authors were holy people
   b) they believe its authors had special powers
   c) they believe its authors were inspired by God
   d) they believe its authors wrote eternal truths

Activities

Complete the answers to these questions:

1 Outline three reasons why non-religious people do not believe in life after death.

Non-religious people do not believe in life after death because life after death depends on there being a God and they do not believe in God. They also ....

A third reason is that ....

2 Explain two reasons why Christians reject arguments against life after death. In your answer you must refer to a source of wisdom and authority.

Christians reject arguments against life after death because they believe the Bible evidence for life after death is totally trustworthy because the Bible is inspired by God. The Catechism of the Catholic Church says that ....

Another reason is because the disciples must have been certain that Jesus rose from the dead because ....

Exam support

You might be asked to evaluate a statement such as:

Believing in life after death doesn't make sense in the modern world.

The table below might help you answer such a question.

Arguments for	Arguments against
Life after death assumes that the mind or soul can survive without the body, but the evidence of science is that the human mind is totally dependent on the physical brain.	For life to end at death does not make sense. A life after death, in which people will be judged on how they live this life, with the good rewarded and the evil punished, makes sense of this life.
Space exploration has shown there is no heaven above the sky and physics has shown there is no non-material world on earth, so where could life after death take place?	Belief gives comfort when a loved one dies, because it can seem impossible to believe that they are gone forever.
If there is a non-material afterlife, how would we recognise souls without bodies? If souls survive death, then they would be alone, with no way of contacting other souls.	The idea of an afterlife, where the evil are punished and the good rewarded, makes sense of people's belief in justice and fair play.
Karl Marx said belief in life after death was an invention of the ruling class to be used to keep the working class happy with low wages and poor living conditions.	The idea of an afterlife corresponds with people's religious beliefs.

Topic 1.4.7 Euthanasia

REVISED

Euthanasia means providing a gentle and easy death to someone suffering from a painful, terminal disease who has a poor **quality of life**, by **assisted suicide, voluntary euthanasia** and **non-voluntary euthanasia**.

Christian attitudes to euthanasia

All Christians believe euthanasia is wrong, but they have slightly different attitudes.

Most Christians, including Catholics, ban the three types of euthanasia shown above but accept that advances in modern medicine means that passive euthanasia is not wrong. They believe this because:

- The sanctity of life means it is up to God, not humans, when people die and euthanasia means putting oneself on a par with God, which is forbidden in the Bible.
- Euthanasia is murder, which is forbidden in the Ten Commandments.
- They believe that switching off life-support machines is simply accepting what God has already decided.
- It is acceptable not to give **extraordinary treatment** as it is likely to affect the dignity of dying.

Some Christians (mainly Evangelical Protestants) regard even passive euthanasia as wrong because:

- switching off a life-support machine, for example, means life is being ended by humans, not God
- life is created by God and it is up to God, not humans, when people die.

Some Liberal Christians agree with euthanasia in certain circumstances, such as **living wills**, because they give people a chance to be in control of what doctors are doing to them, which is a basic human right.

Atheist and Humanist attitudes to euthanasia

Some want euthanasia to remain illegal because:

- there is always likely to be doubt as to whether euthanasia is what the person really wants
- a disease might not be terminal, a cure might be found or the patient may go into **remission**
- it is the role of doctors to save lives, not end them.

Others believe that euthanasia should be legalised because:

- advances in medicine have led to people being kept alive who should have died, and whose quality of life is very poor
- if doctors can switch off life-support and stop treatments, why not let them end suffering in a painless way

Christian responses to those who are dying

A major Christian response to the problems of the **terminally ill** has been the hospice movement. Christians believe that instead of euthanasia, the terminally ill should be helped by hospices which aim to relieve and control the pain of the dying (known as **palliative care**). They also help patients, families and friends face up to death. Christian hospices were begun by Dame Cicely Saunders, who founded St Christopher's Hospice in 1967 and many Christians volunteer at hospices.

Extraordinary treatment – treatment which has major effects on the patient and which is likely to prolong life for only a short time

Non-voluntary euthanasia – ending someone's life painlessly when they are unable to ask, but you have good reason for thinking they would want you to do so

Palliative care – medical or nursing care that reduces pain and improves the quality of life of those who have terminal illnesses

Quality of life – the idea that life must have some benefits for it to be worth living

Remission – when a patient with a disease gets better

Terminal illness – an incurable illness leading to death

Voluntary euthanasia – ending life painlessly when someone in great pain asks for death

Sources of wisdom and authority

- The Book of Job says that you cannot accept good from God and refuse to accept trouble.
- The Catechism says that use of painkillers to relieve the suffering of the dying, knowing it will shorten their life, is acceptable because death is not being intended.

Now test yourself

TESTED

1 Ending someone's life painlessly, when they are unable to ask, but you have good reason for thinking they would want you to do so, is:
   a) assisted suicide
   b) non-voluntary euthanasia
   c) lawful euthanasia
   d) voluntary euthanasia
2 Ending life painlessly when someone in great pain asks for death is:
   a) assisted suicide
   b) non-voluntary euthanasia
   c) lawful euthanasia
   d) voluntary euthanasia
3 Quality of life means:
   a) an assessment of whether a patient has enough help to live at home
   b) how good a standard of living a patient has
   c) the idea that life must have some benefits for it to be worth living
   d) the idea that everyone should have a certain standard of living

Activities

Complete the answers to these questions:

1 Outline three types of euthanasia.

One type is passive euthanasia, which includes things like not giving extraordinary treatments to patients with terminal or life-threatening illnesses.

Another type is ....

A third type is ....

2 Explain two reasons why Christians have different views about euthanasia. In your answer you must refer to a source of wisdom and authority.

Most Christians, including Catholics, are against euthanasia because one of the Ten Commandments forbids murder. However, they believe passive euthanasia is not wrong because, for example, painkillers are only intended to remove pain and hastening the person's death is an unintended effect (the doctrine of double effect) and so is not euthanasia.

Some Christians (mainly Evangelical Protestants) regard all such things as euthanasia because ....

....

Exam support

You might be asked to evaluate a statement such as:

People dying in agony should be offered euthanasia.

The table below might help you answer such a question.

Arguments for	Arguments against
It is a basic human right to have control over your body and what people do to it. People have a right to refuse medical treatment and should have a right to ask for euthanasia.	Genesis says life was created by God and so it is sacred to God. Only God, not humans, has the right to decide when people die.
People should have the right to die when they are in agony and have no quality of life.	Any form of euthanasia means life is being ended by humans, not God, which is wrong.
Christians may feel that euthanasia is obeying Jesus' command to love their neighbour who is suffering.	Any form of euthanasia is murder, which is banned by God in the Ten Commandments.
Suicide is no longer illegal and people should have the right to ask doctors to assist their suicide if they are too ill to do it alone.	Christians should follow the teaching of the Book of Job that says we should accept whatever sufferings are sent to us.

Topic 1.4.8 The natural world

REVISED

The Genesis creation story says God gave humans stewardship of the earth by giving them control of animals. However, the Old Testament teaches that humans must treat animals humanely and treat the land kindly. Jesus taught that God expects humans to pass on to the next generation more than they have been given and that Christians must share the earth's resources fairly.

Threats to the natural world

Pollution, such as acid rain, damages buildings, while human waste in the form of litter and sewage damages the **environment** and causes major health problems.

Global warming could result in some coastal towns disappearing under water as a result of a rise in sea level. Increases in carbon emissions due to the burning of fossil fuels has led to the '**greenhouse effect**' causing a rise in the earth's temperature.

Renewable resources are those that can be used repeatedly because they renew themselves. They include wind power, solar power and water power, as well as fertile land which is used to produce food and biofuels and soft woods which grow quickly and so are replaced.

Finite resources (non-renewable resources) such as oil, coal, metals and hard woods disappear once they are used and this will cause humans major problems.

Christian responses

The responsibility to be God's stewards and to leave the earth a better place than they found it means that Christians should try to:

- reduce pollution by: recycling, promoting the use of waste to produce electricity and encouraging people not to drop litter
- reduce global warming by: using energy efficient technologies, promoting renewable energy sources, using and promoting public transport, opposing deforestation
- reduce the problem of scarce resources by: recycling, using renewable resources to produce electricity, encouraging the use of electric cars, producing plastics from plants rather than oil.

Animal rights

This is the idea that the basic interests of non-human animals should be given the same consideration as those of humans.

Some Christians believe animals should not be used for food or research because:

- all animals are made by God and so are just as valuable as humans
- Jesus' teachings seem to imply that animals are valuable to God
- the benefits of animals for research are not justified by the cruelty involved
- using animals for food is a waste of resources.

Most Christians support using animals for food and research because:

- only humans were made in the image of God and so are special
- Genesis says God put mankind in charge of animals to use for human benefit
- animal testing has produced vaccines which have wiped out deadly diseases
- the use of animals for food is why God produced the food chain, as shown in Genesis 1–3.

Environment – the surroundings in which plants and animals live and on which they depend for survival

Finite resources – resources which can only be used once, for example oil, metals

Greenhouse effect – the carbon dioxide from burned fossil fuels creates a barrier in the same way as the glass in a greenhouse: it allows the sun's heat through, but then traps it, causing the temperature to rise

Renewable resources – resources which do not run out, for example hydroelectric power from water

Stewardship – looking after something so it can be passed on to the next generation

Sources of wisdom and authority

- Genesis says God put mankind in charge of animals to use for human benefit.
- The Catechism of the Catholic Church says that God granted humans dominion over nature, but this is limited by the need to guard the quality of life for our neighbours.
- In Genesis God says to humans, 'everything that lives and moves will be food for you' (Genesis 9:3).
- The Church of England leaders have permitted the use of animals for research.

Now test yourself

TESTED

1 Resources which can only be used once are called:
   a) renewable resources
   b) eternal resources
   c) finite resources
   d) infinite resources
2 Resources which do not run out are called:
   a) renewable resources
   b) eternal resources
   c) finite resources
   d) infinite resources
3 Looking after something so it can be passed on to the next generation is called:
   a) management
   b) regency
   c) stewardship
   d) administration

Activities

Complete the answers to these questions:

1 Outline three threats to the environment.

Global warming is a threat to the environment because it causes flooding. Another threat is pollution which causes health problems. A third threat is ……………………

2 Explain two reasons why Christians work to conserve the environment. In your answer you must refer to a source of wisdom and authority.

Christians work to conserve the environment because Genesis teaches that God made humans stewards of the earth and that they will be judged on how well they fulfil that task. The Catholic Catechism on Nature says that ……………………

Christians also work to conserve the environment because ……………………

Exam support

You might be asked to evaluate a statement such as:

Animals cannot have rights.

The table below might help you answer such a question.

Arguments for	Arguments against
Animals don't think and do not behave morally.	All animals are made by God and so are just as intrinsically valuable as humans.
Animals are not able to make moral choices.	Animals can suffer and so they should have the right not to be treated cruelly.
Only humans were made in the image of God and so are special because they have a soul.	Animals can experience pleasure, fear, frustration, loneliness and familial love, and should have the right for these needs to be taken into consideration by humans in their treatment of animals.
Genesis says God put mankind in charge of animals to use for human benefit.	The way animals react when humans treat them badly shows they have the right for their needs to be taken into account.

2.1 Muslim beliefs

Topic 2.1.1 The six beliefs of Islam

REVISED

Sunni Muslims believe that there are six articles of faith which a Muslim must believe to be accepted as a Muslim: belief in Allah, belief in his angels, belief in his holy books, belief in his messengers, belief in the Last Day and belief in life after death.

The first five beliefs are based on verses from the Qur'an, but the full six are based on a **hadith** of the Prophet Muhammad. Hadith are second in authority to the Qur'an for Sunni Muslims because they believe Muhammad was the final prophet so his words must be important. Hadith are one of the bases of the **Shari'ah**.

Sunni Muslims often describe the six beliefs as ***Tawhid*** (the unity of Allah) – belief in Allah, ***Risalah*** (the messengers of Allah) – belief in angels, holy books and messengers and ***Akirah*** (the last things) – belief in the Last Day and life after death.

The six beliefs are very important for Sunni Muslims because:

1. They summarise the Muslim faith.
2. Believing in *Tawhid* shows that Muslims believe God is the only one, the all-powerful creator, who is the same God worshipped by Jews and Christians.
3. Believing in angels shows that God can communicate with humans via his special beings.
4. Believing in the prophets of God shows that Islam is both the first religion (it began with the Prophet Adam) and the last religion (the final prophet is Muhammad).
5. Believing in the holy books of God shows that God has sent books to show humans what to believe and how to live. It also shows that the holy books given to Jews and Christians were distorted, and that the Qur'an is God's final word to humanity, given in a form that can never be distorted.
6. Believing in *Akirah* means people will be judged by Allah at the Last Day and sent to heaven or hell on the basis of how they have lived their lives.

Akirah – belief in the Last Day and life after death

Hadith – sayings of the Prophet Muhammad

Risalah – belief in Allah's angels, prophets and holy books

Shari'ah – the holy law of Islam which covers all aspects of life

Tawhid – the belief in Allah's unity

The six beliefs in Muslim communities today

Most Sunni Muslim communities believe that the six beliefs mean that:

- All people are created equal in the sight of Allah. No one is superior to another except because of their piety and righteousness. No one should be judged on their gender, colour, ethnicity or disabilities.
- In Islam there are no priests, priesthood or holy men with special authority. The only intermediaries between God and humans are angels, and since belief in *Risalah* means there can be no prophets after Muhammad, no humans can have God's special authority.
- People are born free of any sin and bear no responsibility for the faults and sins of other people. Only after reaching the age of puberty can people be held responsible for their actions in this life.
- Salvation comes through believing the six beliefs and living the Muslim life as set out in the Qur'an and hadith.

Sources of wisdom and authority

- A hadith of the Prophet says that Muslims must believe in Allah, his angels, his holy books, his Messengers, in the Last Day and life after death.
- The Qur'an says that those who do not believe in God and his angels and his scriptures and his messengers and the Last Day are not Muslims.

Now test yourself

TESTED

1 Belief in the Last Day and life after death is called:
   a) *Akirah*
   b) *Tawhid*
   c) *Risalah*
   d) Hadith
2 The sayings of the Prophet Muhammad are called:
   a) *Akirah*
   b) *Tawhid*
   c) *Risalah*
   d) Hadith
3 Belief in Allah's angels, prophets and holy books is called:
   a) *Akirah*
   b) *Tawhid*
   c) *Risalah*
   d) Hadith
4 Belief in Allah's unity is called:
   a) *Akirah*
   b) *Tawhid*
   c) *Risalah*
   d) Hadith

Activities

Complete the answers to these questions:

1 Outline three of the six beliefs of Islam.

Muslims believe in God's unity. They also believe in God's angels and prophets. A third belief is ....

....

2 Explain two reasons why the six beliefs are important for Muslims. In your answer you must refer to a source of wisdom and authority.

The six beliefs are important to Muslims because they summarise the Muslim faith and tell Muslims what they must believe. They are based on verses from the Qur'an, the holy book of Islam, and from a hadith of Muhammad himself which says, ...

Another reason the beliefs are important is because ....

....

Exam support

You might be asked to evaluate a statement such as:

If you believe the six beliefs, you are a Muslim.

The table below might help you answer such a question.

Arguments for	Arguments against
Muhammad said the six beliefs are what Muslims have to believe.	Islam is about how you behave as well as what you believe.
If you believe the six beliefs, you believe in God, the one, the all-powerful creator.	Sunni Islam has Five Pillars which you have to practise to be a Muslim.
If you believe the six beliefs, you believe that Muhammad is God's final prophet and example of how to live.	Islam is a way of life and you need to follow the Shari'ah to be a Muslim.
If you believe the six beliefs, you believe the Qur'an is God's final word to humans.	Whether you believe or not, if you eat pork, drink alcohol or lend money at interest, you are not a proper Muslim.

Topic 2.1.2 The five roots in Shi'a Islam

REVISED

Shi'a Muslims have the five roots of faith (***Usul ad-Din***) rather than the six beliefs as the basis of their faith:

1 Belief in the oneness of Allah (*Tawhid*) and all Allah's characteristics that come from his oneness.
2 Belief in Allah's justice (***Adalat***) – the universe works according to laws established by Allah and the way it operates is fair and just.
3 Belief in Allah's prophets from Adam to Muhammad.
4 Belief in the successors of Muhammad (**Imams**) – belief that the chosen descendants of the Prophet Muhammad were given special powers by Allah. These Imams are the ones who determine what the Qur'an means and what the law should be (most Shi'as believe there have been Twelve Imams – referred to as Twelvers). Today specially able religious leaders (**mujtahids** or **ayatollahs**) do this job.
5 Belief in the Day of Judgement, with judgement being based on believing the five roots and following the Shi'a Shari'ah.

The five roots developed in order to sum up what one must believe to be a Shi'a Muslim and to express in simple terms which beliefs differentiate Shi'a Muslims from Sunni Muslims.

The five roots are important because:

- they are the basis of Shi'a Islam; it is from the roots that the religion grows
- they are the five principles of faith and show a person what they must believe to be a Shi'a Muslim
- they come from the teachings of the Qur'an and the Twelve Imams which means they are of utmost importance to Shi'a Muslims
- Shi'a Muslims believe that unless they understand and believe the five roots, they will not be able to perform the acts of worship necessary to live the Muslim life
- they are the beliefs that Muslims must hold if their practices are to be correct and ensure that they go to heaven.

Most Sunni Muslims have never heard of the five roots but they accept roots 1, 2, 3 and 5 as they are the same as the six beliefs. Root 4 is the essential difference between Sunni and Shi'a Muslims.

There are many different **sects** within Shi'a Islam and their origins have led to the five roots having different levels of importance, in particular the fourth root about the successor of Muhammad.

Most Shi'as are Twelvers, that is they believe there were twelve imams after Muhammad and the twelfth went into hiding (the Hidden Imam) and is in contact with Shi'a leaders.

The **Ismaili** Shi'as (Seveners) believe that the seventh imam, Isma'il, was the final Imam. The Nizari Khoja branch of Ismailis believe that the Imamate continued from Isma'il to the present day, and that their current leader, the Agha Khan, is the Imam.

The **Ahmadiyya**, who developed from Ismailis in Pakistan 150 years ago, accept the Sunni six beliefs rather than the Shi'a five roots, although they believe their founder, Mirza Ahmad, received a special message.

Adalat – God's attribute of justice

Ahmadiyya – a Muslim sect founded in Pakistan by Yirza Ahmad

Ayatollah – the highest ranking religious leader in Twelver Shi'ism

Imam – for Shi'as, successor of the Prophet Muhammad, but 'imam' with a small 'i' is a prayer leader for Sunnis

Ismaili – Shi'as who believe the seventh Imam, Isma'il, was the final Imam

Mujtahid – a Shi'a scholar with sufficient training and knowledge to interpret the Shari'ah

Sect – group with different religious beliefs from those of a larger group to which they belong

Usul ad-Din – the five roots of Shi'ah Islam

Sources of wisdom and authority

There is a Shi'a hadith which says that if you do not know the Imam of the age, you will die a heathen.

Now test yourself

TESTED

1 God's attribute of justice is:
a) ayatollah
b) *Adalat*
c) Imam
d) mujtahid

2 The highest ranking religious leader in Twelver Shi'ism is:
a) ayatollah
b) *Adalat*
c) Imam
d) mujtahid

3 Successors of the Prophet Muhammad for Shi'as are known as:
a) ayatollah
b) *Adalat*
c) Imam
d) mujtahid

4 Shi'a scholars with sufficient training and knowledge to interpret the Shari'ah are known as:
a) ayatollah
b) *Adalat*
c) Imam
d) mujtahid

Activities

Complete the answers to these questions:

1 Outline three of the five roots of Shi'a Islam.

The first root is belief in God's oneness. Another root is belief in God's justice. Another root is ....

....

2 Explain two reasons why the five roots are important for Shi'a Muslims. In your answer you must refer to a source of wisdom and authority.

The five roots are important for Shi'a Muslims because they show what Shi'as must believe to be true Shi'a Muslims. They also show what differentiates Shi'a Muslims from Sunni Muslims, especially root 4, which sums up Shi'a belief in the Imams. Indeed, there is a Shi'a hadith which says that if you do not know the Imam of the age, you will die a heathen.

The five roots are also important because, ...

Exam support

You might be asked to evaluate a statement such as:

It doesn't matter what you believe as long as you worship God and live a good life.

The table below might help you answer such a question.

Arguments for	Arguments against
Muslims believe God is all-merciful, all-compassionate, so if people are worshipping him, he won't condemn them for choosing the wrong way.	What you believe determines what living a good life is, so it therefore does matter what you believe.
Shi'a Muslims believe in God's justice and a just God must approve of people who are living a good life and worshipping God as best they can.	Sunni Muslims believe there can be no prophets after Muhammad and think those who believe in the Imams won't get to heaven as they have denied Muhammad being the seal of the prophets.
What you believe is often determined by how you've been brought up and you cannot change that, so it cannot matter to God.	Shi'a Muslims think those who don't believe in the Imams are rejecting God's chosen ones and so won't get to heaven.
What you believe does not harm other people, and if you're living a good life you won't be harming other people.	Many Muslims believe you can only live a good life if you are following the right beliefs.

Topic 2.1.3 The nature of Allah

REVISED

Muslims always refer to God as **Allah** because this is the word used for God in the Qur'an and is the Arabic for God. Allah has no plural form and using it confirms the fundamental Muslim belief that God is the one and only God.

Muslim beliefs about Allah's nature are found in the Qur'an (especially the ninety-nine names) which Muslims believe is God's actual words to humanity.

The main characteristics of God revealed in the Qur'an are:

- Oneness (***Tawhid***) – this is the basis of Islam. Allah's unity means he has no partners, no helpers and especially no equals. Muslims feel that the Christian belief in God as a Trinity, and in Jesus as the Son of God, is an insult to Allah's unity.
- Omnipotence – Allah has created the universe and so must have complete power over it. Islam means submission to God's will and a Muslim is one who has submitted their will to God's will because God is so great.
- Beneficence and mercy – every **surah** except Surah 9 begins with the ***bismillah***: 'In the name of Allah, the Merciful, the Compassionate'. His mercy is shown in the way he sent prophets to show people how to live and will forgive them if they fail in their attempts to live the perfect Muslim life.
- Justice (*Adalat*) – Allah's justice is shown in the way the universe works and in the holy law, the **Shari'ah**, Allah has given to make sure that humans deal fairly and justly with each other.
- Allah's transcendence and immanence – Allah is totally beyond the material and so beyond human experience, and yet is close to humans and can be contacted by humans because of his immanence. Transcendence and immanence are a great mystery: God is both far beyond humans and yet also close to them.

Allah – the Arabic for God

Bismillah – the words at the beginning of each surah (except Surah 9), 'In the name of Allah, the Merciful, the Compassionate'

Shari'ah – the holy law of Islam

Shirk – the sin of associating other things with God; it is the worst sin

Surah – a chapter of the Qur'an (there are 114 surahs)

Tawhid – God's unity

Ummah – the Muslim community

Why the characteristics of Allah are important for Muslims

- *Tawhid* means that one God created everything and so Muslims must try to preserve the oneness of nature. This also means the Muslim community itself must be a unity (this is called the ***ummah***) which follows one law, the Shari'ah.
- *Tawhid* also means Muslims must only worship Allah; indeed the worst sin a Muslim can commit is the sin of ***shirk*** which is to associate others with Allah – this is why there are no images or statues in the mosque.
- Allah's omnipotence means Allah is in control of everything that happens.
- Allah's compassion and mercy means Muslims should be merciful and forgiving to those who cause them offence.
- Allah's justice means that Muslims must behave justly to other people and ensure that the world is governed in a fair way by following the Shari'ah.
- Allah's transcendence shows that Allah is worthy of humanity's worship and praise since he is greater than anything.
- Allah's immanence means that Allah is part of the universe he has created and so science and learning can discover Allah and Allah can be contacted by humans.

All Allah's characteristics can be summed up by *Tawhid*. Everything comes from Allah's oneness and unity which is why a Muslim should seek the oneness of humanity and the unity of humans with nature.

Sources of wisdom and authority

- Surah 112 says that God is the one and only God.
- Surah 2 says that God is loving, self-subsisting and eternal.
- Surah 2 says the Qur'an is the book whose guidance is sure.
- Surah 50 says that God is nearer to man than his jugular vein.
- Surah 2 says that God is everywhere and all-powerful.

Now test yourself

TESTED

1 The sin of associating other things with God is called:
a) *bismillah*
b) Shari'ah
c) *shirk*
d) *ummah*

2 The Muslim community is known as:
a) *bismillah*
b) Shari'ah
c) *shirk*
d) *ummah*

3 The words at the beginning of each surah are called:
a) *bismillah*
b) Shari'ah
c) *shirk*
d) *ummah*

4 The holy law of Islam is called:
a) *bismillah*
b) Shari'ah
c) *shirk*
d) *ummah*

Activities

Complete the answers to these questions:

1 Outline three Muslim beliefs about the nature of Allah.

Muslims believe that there is only one God and that he is the one and only God.

They also believe that Allah is ....

They also believe that ....

2 Explain two reasons why God's unity is important for Muslims. In your answer you must refer to a source of wisdom and authority.

God's unity is known as Tawhid, meaning that one God created everything. This means Muslims must try to preserve the oneness of nature and the Muslim community must itself be a unity (ummah) following one law, the Shari'ah.

Tawhid also means Muslims must only worship Allah, because as Surah 112 says, ...

Exam support

You might be asked to evaluate a statement such as:

No one can say what God is like.

The table below might help you answer such a question.

Arguments for	Arguments against
God is transcendent and so is far beyond human understanding.	The Qur'an is God's word and it tells us what God is like.
God is infinite and humans are finite beings, so we cannot know what God is like.	The Qur'an has ninety-nine names of God to tell humans what God is like.
No one has seen God so we cannot know what God is like.	Muhammad was chosen by God to be his final prophet and he gave many hadith, telling us what God is like.
No one can prove that what the Qur'an or any other holy book says about God is true.	God is merciful and compassionate and so wants humans to know what he is like.

Topic 2.1.4 *Risalah* (prophets)

REVISED

Muslims believe Allah created humans to look after the earth for him (Allah's ***khalifahs*** or **vicegerents**) and they need prophets to know how to do this.

Islam teaches that the prophets were all ordinary humans, who were only special because they were chosen to receive Allah's messages. All the prophets except Isa were married and had children. Each prophet brought Islam in its perfect form but their message was ignored, distorted or forgotten and so Allah had to send new prophets.

The main prophets of Islam

- Adam was the first prophet of Islam created by Allah to look after the earth. The devil (Iblis) tempted Adam and his wife to disobey Allah and they were sent to earth where Allah forgave them and gave Adam his guidance as the first prophet. According to the hadith, Adam built the first House for Allah (**Ka'aba**) in **Makkah** (Mecca) to thank Allah.
- Ibrahim (Abraham) was the greatest of the prophets before Isa (Jesus). Ibrahim rejected the polytheism (worshipping many gods) of his family, condemned their idolatry and showed them the truth of Islam. Ibrahim restored the Ka'aba after it had been destroyed and established it as a place of pilgrimage Ibrahim was given the first holy book of Sahifa Ibrahim (the Scrolls of Abraham).
- Isma'il, Ibrahim's son, helped his father rebuild the Ka'aba and is regarded as the prophet to the Arabs. Muslims believe him to be the ancestor of Muhammad.
- Musa (Moses) was born a Jew, according to the Qur'an, but brought up by Pharaoh's wife. Allah called him to lead the Jews out of slavery in Egypt and into God's promised land. Musa was given the holy book of Tawrat (Torah), but the people distorted or rejected his message.
- Dawud (David), the great King of Israel, was chosen as a prophet and given the holy book of Zabur (Psalms) because of the distortion of the Tawrat.
- Isa (Jesus) is a major figure in the Qur'an, which says he had a virgin birth and performed many miracles. The Qur'an claims that Allah stopped the Jews from executing and crucifying him and raised Isa to Himself so that he never died. Isa was given the holy book Injil (Gospel), but the Qur'an insists he was only an ordinary man and a prophet, not the son of God.
- Muhammad was called by Allah to bring his final message in a holy book (the Qur'an) which could never be distorted. Muhammad is the seal of the prophets (acting like the seal put on a letter to prove who it came from and to make sure nothing could be added). As the seal, Muhammad is the final prophet and therefore the perfect example for Muslims.

Muslims believe that:

- Every prophet was called by Allah and given Allah's true message to give to the people of earth and so their teachings should be followed.
- Prophets were just ordinary human beings.
- The Qur'an is the final unalterable word of God.
- Muhammad received the final message from Allah so Islam is both the first and the last religion.
- Muhammad was the final prophet, and so good Muslims should follow his **Sunnah** because his was the last example of how to live.

Ka'aba – the shrine in Makkah which Muslims face to say prayers and which is the centre of *hajj*

Khalifahs – Allah's stewards or vicegerents

Makkah – the city in Arabia where Muhammad was born

Sunnah – the example and way of life of the Prophet Muhammad

Vicegerent – a person appointed to look after things on behalf of a ruler

Sources of wisdom and authority

- The Qur'an says that Abraham was neither a Jew nor a Christian, but true in the faith of Islam.
- The Qur'an says that Moses was a specially chosen messenger and prophet.
- The Qur'an says that Christ, the son of Mary, was a human being and no more than an apostle.
- Surah 33 says that Muhammad is the apostle of God, and the seal of the prophets.

Now test yourself

TESTED

1 Muslims call Jesus:
   a) Isma'il
   b) Isa
   c) Ka'aba
   d) *khalifah*
2 The word for Allah's steward or vicegerent is:
   a) Isma'il
   b) Isa
   c) Ka'aba
   d) *khalifah*
3 Ibrahim's son, the father of the Arab peoples, is called:
   a) Isma'il
   b) Isa
   c) Ka'aba
   d) *khalifah*
4 The shrine which Muslims face to say prayers is called:
   a) Isma'il
   b) Isa
   c) Ka'aba
   d) *khalifah*

Activities

Complete the answers to these questions:

1 Outline three Muslims beliefs about prophets.

Muslims believe that prophets are human. They believe that prophets are specially chosen to receive Allah's message, Islam, in its perfect form.

Muslims also believe ....

2 Explain two beliefs which the prophets teach Muslims. In your answer you must refer to a source of wisdom and authority.

The prophets teach Muslims that Muhammad was the final prophet, so good Muslims should follow the Sunnah of the Prophet Muhammad, which is the final example of how to live. As Surah 33 says, ...

....

They also teach Muslims that the prophets were just ordinary human beings and so Muslims should have nothing to do with religions which claim any sort of divine status for their leaders.

Exam support

You might be asked to evaluate a statement such as: *Prophets show how much God loves humanity.*

The table below might help you answer such a question.

Arguments for	Arguments against
God chose ordinary people to be prophets and each was given Allah's message in the form of a holy book, which was God's guide on how people should live their lives.	The prophets were only sent to Jewish and Arab peoples in the Middle East; Allah did not send any prophets to Europe, America or the Far East.
When people ignored or distorted Allah's message, instead of punishing them he sent another prophet.	God sent his final word in Arabic which most people can't understand.
Allah told his prophets to give people clear guidance on what to do to go to heaven after death.	All the prophets said those who did not obey God's word would go to hell, even if they had no chance to hear or understand it.
God sent Muhammad with the Qur'an so that people would have a final example as well as his final word to show them how to live.	If God really loved all humanity, some of the prophets would have been women as they represent 50 per cent of humanity.

Topic 2.1.5 Muslim holy books (kitub)

REVISED

- Prophet Ibrahim was given the message in a book called **Sahifa Ibrahim** (the Scrolls of Abraham). However, this book became so distorted that all copies were lost.
- Prophet Musa (Moses) was given the message in the holy book known as **Tawrat** (Torah). Although Musa's message became distorted, some parts remained in the Old Testament, which is why many elements of Judaism (including the food laws) are still very similar to Islam.
- Prophet Dawud was given the message in the **Zabur** (Psalms), some of which have survived undistorted in the Psalms of the Old Testament.
- Prophet Isa (Jesus) was given the **Injil** (Gospel) which he then preached to the Jewish people. Muslims believe the Injil was not the same as the New Testament or the four Gospels; instead, these are human records of what people remembered of the true Gospel preached by Isa (for example, the New Testament says Isa was God's son when he was really the prophet of God). Muslims also believe Christians removed from the Injil prophecies about the coming of Muhammad.
- Allah decided that his message had to be given in a new way because he had sent it with the other prophets and each time it had been distorted or disobeyed. Prophet Muhammad was given the Qur'an in a way that could not be distorted: because Muhammad could not read or write God gave him the message as a dictation which he learnt by heart and recited to the people. Later Muhammad had secretaries who wrote down the revelations. Muhammad then checked they were accurate and sorted the revelations into surahs.

Muslims disagree about the exact nature of the holy books:

- Most Muslims believe that God made one holy book, the Qur'an, which is his eternal word and each holy book given to a prophet was simply a copy of that 'heavenly original'.
- Some Muslim scholars believe that the earlier holy books only contained certain parts of the Qur'an, which was why they could be distorted. Only Muhammad was given God's full eternal word in the undistortable Qur'an.

How the Qur'an came to us

- When Muhammad died, the first Caliph, decided that it was essential for there to be an authorised version of the revelations and used Muhammad's chief secretary to do this.
- The authorised version was finalised by the third Caliph, **Uthman**, so that now all Qur'ans have the same surahs, words and letters.
- Uthman organised the Qur'an by length of surah so that Surah 2 is the longest and Surah 114 the shortest (Surah 1 is a call to prayer).

The significance of Muslim beliefs about holy books

Muslim beliefs about the holy books revealed before Muhammad received the Qur'an show that:

- God has always made sure people knew what to believe and how to live
- The old books have been distorted and so are no longer God's word,
- The Jewish Tenakh and the Christian Bible are not holy books for most Muslims

Muslims believe that the way the Qur'an was revealed to Muhammad and then compiled by the Caliphs guarantees that the Arabic Qur'an, as used by Muslims today, is the exact words of God revealed to Muhammad. This is why Muslims believe the Qur'an is holy and never touch it without first washing their hands. It is also why they obey what the Qur'an says.

Injil – the Gospel given to Isa (Jesus)

Kitub – holy books (singular *kitab*)

Sahifa Ibrahim – the holy book given to Ibrahim (Abraham)

Tawrat – the holy book given to Musa (Moses)

Uthman – the third Caliph, who ordered the final official copy of the Qur'an

Zabur – the holy book given to Dawud (David)

Sources of wisdom and authority

- Surah 4 says that God gave Abraham the Book and Wisdom.
- Surah 11 says that God gave Moses the Book of Tawrat.
- Surah 5 says that God gave Jesus the Gospel (Injil).
- The first revelation of the Qur'an was: 'Proclaim (recite) in the name of thy Lord and Cherisher who created.' (Surah 96:1)

Now test yourself

TESTED

1 The Arabic word for holy books is:
   a) Kitab
   b) Injil
   c) Zabur
   d) Tawrat

2 The holy book given to Isa (Jesus) is called:
   a) Kitab
   b) Injil
   c) Zabur
   d) Tawrat

3 The holy book given to Musa (Moses) is called:
   a) Kitab
   b) Injil
   c) Zabur
   d) Tawrat

4 The holy book given to Dawud (David) is called:
   a) Kitab
   b) Injil
   c) Zabur
   d) Tawrat

Activities

Complete the answers to these questions:

1 Outline three Muslim holy books.

The holy book given to the Prophet Ibrahim (Abraham) is known as Sahifa Ibrahim or Scrolls of Abraham.

Another Muslim holy book is ....

A third holy book is ....

2 Explain two reasons why there are Muslim holy books other than the Qur'an. In your answer you must refer to a source of wisdom and authority.

Muslims believe that God sent prophets with his message and the most important of these were given God's holy book so that Muslims would know what to believe and how to live. Adam was the first to receive God's book, but humans subsequently distorted God's words and so God had to send other messengers.

The Qur'an says that ....

....

As a result, God had to send Muhammad the Qur'an in a form that could never be distorted.

Exam support

You might be asked to evaluate a statement such as:

The Qur'an is God's final word to humanity and so should be obeyed.

The table below might help you answer such a question.

Arguments for	Arguments against
Muhammad must have received the Qur'an from God because he could not read or write.	Shi'a Muslims believe that God has sent further messages through the Imams.
The Qur'an itself says that it is God's word.	God cannot have said everything that needed saying 1,400 years ago. Times have changed and he must be able to give messages to people today.
The Qur'an must be God's final word because it has never been changed – all Qur'ans have the same number of surahs, Arabic words and Arabic letters.	If the Qur'an was God's final word, he would have given it in a language he knew most people would speak – Chinese or English, not Arabic.
If the Qur'an is God's final word to humans, then humans should obey it because God should be obeyed.	There is no proof the Qur'an is God's word – if Muhammad could not read, how did he know his secretaries wrote the right words down?

Topic 2.1.6 *Malaikah* (angels)

REVISED

The nature of angels

Muslims believe that the unity and greatness of Allah mean that he is far too holy to be able to communicate directly with humans and so he created angels (***malaikah***). The Qur'an teaches that because angels have no free will, they obey all Allah's commands and so never commit sins. As they are sinless, angels can have direct contact with Allah and pass his messages to humans.

The Qur'an teaches that when he created Adam, Allah ordered the angels to bow down to him. Iblis (**Shaytan**) was an angel who refused to bow down to Adam and so was cast out of heaven and set up his own kingdom of hell. The Qur'an says that Iblis begged Allah to postpone his punishment for disobedience until the Last Day, which is why Iblis is able to tempt humans to go against Allah.

Muslims believe that angels have many functions:

- They praise Allah in heaven.
- They are the guardians of the gates of hell.
- They record the good and bad deeds of humans to present to Allah on the Last Day as the basis for his judgement.

The main angels are:

- **Jibril** (Gabriel) – the chief angel whose main role is to deliver Allah's message to the prophets so that they could pass it on to humanity. Jibril told the prophet Ibrahim about the births of Ishaq and Isma'il. He also told Zechariah about the birth of **Yahya** (John the Baptist) and **Maryam** (Mary) about the birth of Isa. Jibril's most important role was to reveal the Qur'an to Muhammad. While Muhammad was meditating in a cave near Makkah, Jibril appeared with the first revelation of the Qur'an. Jibril continued to give Muhammad revelations for the next twenty years until the Qur'an was complete.
- **Mika'il** (Michael) – the second most important angel, he is believed to be the guardian of heaven, protecting it from evil and the devil. Mika'il also ensures that humans are nourished by sending rain to the earth.
- **Izra'il** – the angel of death. The Qur'an says that the angel of death takes the souls of people at death and returns them to Allah. There are hadith which record that the prophets met Izra'il during their lives and that Izra'il watches over the dying.

Why angels are important for Muslims

- Allah is so great and holy that he cannot communicate directly with humans.
- Allah loves his creation and has sent angels with his message so that if humans follow the message, they will go to heaven.
- Although his angels perform work for him, Allah is in ultimate control of human destiny.
- Everything humans do is known to Allah; the recording angels mean humans cannot hide anything from Allah.
- Humans need to follow the message sent by Jibril if they are to enter heaven.

Izra'il – the angel of death

Jibril – the angel Gabriel

Malaikah – angels

Maryam – the Virgin Mary

Mika'il – the angel Michael

Shaytan – the devil

Yahya – John the Baptist

Sources of wisdom and authority

- Surah 35 says that God made the angels to be his messengers.
- Surah 50 says everyone has two recording angels that record everything people say and do, to be read out on the Day of Judgement.

Now test yourself

TESTED

1 The angel of death is:
   a) Izra'il
   b) *Malaikah*
   c) Jibril
   d) Yahya
2 The angel Gabriel is:
   a) Izra'il
   b) *Malaikah*
   c) Jibril
   d) Yahya
3 Angels are
   a) Izra'il
   b) *Malaikah*
   c) Jibril
   d) Yahya
4 John the Baptist is:
   a) Izra'il
   b) *Malaikah*
   c) Jibril
   d) Yahya

Activities

Complete the answers to these questions:

1 Outline three Muslim beliefs about angels.

Muslims believe that angels praise Allah in heaven. They are also the guardians of the gates of hell.

There are recording angels who ....

2 Explain two reasons why angels are important in Islam. In your answer you must refer to a source of wisdom and authority.

Angels are important because Muslims believe that Allah is too holy and powerful to contact humans and so he needed sinless angels who have no free will to communicate with humans. As Surah 35 says, 'Praise Allah who made the angels his messengers'.

Another reason is because ....

Exam support

You might be asked to evaluate a statement such as:

Without angels there would be no Islam.

The table below might help you answer such a question.

Arguments for	Arguments against
Allah was only able to send messages to the prophets via angels.	God is all-powerful so he must have been able to establish Islam without angels.
Without angels Muhammad would not have been called to become God's final prophet.	God must be able to communicate with humans without angels, otherwise how do they pray to him?
Without angels Muhammad could not have received the revelations that made up the Qur'an.	God could have sent the Qur'an down in book form.
With no Muhammad and no Qur'an, there would have been no Islam.	God could have created other beings to be his messengers.

Topic 2.1.7 *Al-Qadr* (fate)

REVISED

What Muslims believe about *al-Qadr*

Al-Qadr means power or fate or **predestination**, and for Muslims it means that everything in the universe is following a divine plan.

This belief comes from many references in the Qur'an to the way in which things happened in the lives of the prophets, which they did not understand at the time, but which they later came to see were a part of Allah's plan for them. As a result of these verses, Muslims believe that Allah has a plan for the universe, has the power to make that plan happen (Allah is omnipotent), knows what will happen (Allah is omniscient) and in the end everything will work out as Allah willed (wanted). This is why many Muslims will say '***insh Allah***' meaning 'if Allah wills' – things will only happen if Allah wants them to.

Belief in *al-Qadr* seems to conflict with Muslim teachings on *Akirah* which teaches that there will be a final judgement at the end of the world when Allah will judge everyone on the basis of their beliefs and actions and reward or punish them accordingly. However, people can only be punished for actions for which they are responsible and which they could have done differently if they had so chosen. However, *al-Qadr* means everything is part of God's plan, so humans don't really have a choice.

Muslims respond to this problem in two ways:

- Many Shi'a Muslims follow the **Mu'tazilites'** belief that Allah created humans with free will and made them his vicegerents, responsible for the world. So it is up to humans what happens and individual humans are responsible for their actions if misusing their free will results in them disobeying God.
- Sunni Muslims tend to follow the explanation of another eighth-century theologian, al'Ashari, which is that Allah knows what people will do before they do it, since he has the attribute of **foreknowledge**, but that people do it of their own free will.

Belief in *Al-Qadr* means that Allah has a master plan for the universe, and, since Allah is omnipotent, nothing happens without Allah's permission. This means that:

- although Muslims may face present sufferings, they do not need to worry about their long-term future because God is in control, so all will be well
- any sufferings Muslims undergo must be accepted because what they suffer is part of God's plan and so will have an eventual good outcome
- Muslims still have free will and so although God's plans will happen, Muslims have to make their own choices and be responsible for their own actions and destiny
- Muslims need to work out what God wants them to do (for most Muslims this simply means observing the Five Pillars and living according to the Shari'ah) so they can be sure their free choices are what God wants to happen.

Al-Qadr – God's power to make things happen according to his plan

Foreknowledge – knowing what is going to happen long before it does

Insh Allah – if God wills

Mu'tazilites – eighth-century Muslim theologians regarded as non-Muslim by most Sunni Muslims today

Predestination – the belief that everything that happens has already been decided

Sources of wisdom and authority

- Surah 33 says that God is the one who has decided in advance what will happen.
- Surah 13 says that God is the master planner of the world's events.

Now test yourself

TESTED

1 Muslims call God's power to make things happen according to his plan:
   a) *Al-Ashari*
   b) *Al'Jannah*
   c) *Al-Qadr*
   d) *Al-Hijra*

2 The Arabic phrase meaning 'if God wills' is:
   a) *La'Allah*
   b) *insh Allah*
   c) *Rasul-Allah*
   d) *Nabi-Allah*

3 What is the name of the eighth-century Muslim theologians regarded as non-Muslim by most Sunnis today?
   a) Asharites
   b) Ahmadiyya
   c) Mu'tazilites
   d) *malaikah*

4 The belief that everything that happens has already been decided is:
   a) foreknowledge
   b) pre-emption
   c) predestination
   d) prerequisite

Activities

Complete the answers to these questions:

1 Outline three implications of belief about *al-Qadr* for Muslims.

Muslims do not need to worry about their long-term future because God is in control, so all will be well. Another implication is that Muslims cannot leave it to God to sort things out, although God's plans will happen, Muslims must make their own choices. A third implication is ....

....

2 Explain two reasons why Muslims believe in *al-Qadr*. In your answer you must refer to a source of wisdom and authority.

Muslims believe in al-Qadr because of the way in which things happened in the lives of the prophets which they did not understand at the time, but which they later came to see were a part of Allah's plan for them. They also believe in al-Qadr because it is referred to many times in the Qur'an, for example ....

....

Exam support

You might be asked to evaluate a statement such as:

Nothing happens unless God wants it to.

The table below might help you answer such a question.

Arguments for	Arguments against
It is the teaching of *al-Qadr* that God has a plan for the world and the power to make it happen.	If true, it must mean that God wants evil things to happen.
It is the teaching of the Qur'an, which is God's word.	If true, it must mean God wants people to suffer in terrible ways.
Muslims believe God is all-powerful and all-knowing so nothing can happen unless he wants it to.	If things only happen because God wants them to, then it means that humans have no free will and are just God's puppets.
If things happen that God does not want to happen, that means God is not in control, but Muslims believe God is in control so nothing can happen against his will.	Belief that nothing happens unless God wants it to means that there is nothing humans can do to make themselves better – they can only do what God has programmed them to do.

Topic 2.1.8 *Akirah* (Muslim beliefs about life after death)

REVISED

Muslims believe that when people die their body stays in the grave until the Last Day when Isa will return, the angel **Israfil** will sound the trumpet, the world as we know it will disappear and the dead will be raised. Everyone will stand before God on the plain of Arafat to be judged by God. Only good Muslims will pass God's judgement, though many Muslims believe that God, 'the Merciful', 'the Compassionate', will forgive Muslims who have tried their best.

Beliefs about paradise and hell

Heaven is ***al'Jannah*** (the Garden), which all Muslims believe will be a paradise. The Qur'an describes it as 'gardens of perpetual bliss'.

Hell is ***Jahannam***, a place of fire and torture. Most Muslims believe that people will stay in hell forever, but some Muslims believe that bad Muslims will only stay in hell for a short time to be punished for their sins. Some Muslims believe that good followers of other religions will only be in hell for a short time too.

Beliefs about death and the Last Day

Muslims have a varity of beliefs about what happens in the period between death and the body being raised on the Last Day (a time known as ***Barzakh***):

- Some believe that souls are visited by the angel of death and questioned about their faith. If they give a good Muslim answer, they are shown their place in heaven, but if not, they are beaten with clubs until the Last Day.
- Others believe that after the death of the body, the soul hovers over the grave until the Last Day.
- Some believe that after death the soul sleeps until the Last Day so that *Barzakh* will just seem like a moment.
- A few Muslims claim that the afterlife is spiritual and that people's souls are judged immediately after death before going to heaven or hell.

Life after death is important for Muslims because:

- the Qur'an teaches that there is life after death
- Muhammad, the final prophet, taught that there is life after death
- belief in life after death is one of the six fundamental beliefs of Sunni Islam and the five roots of Shi'a Islam and Muhammad said all Muslims must believe these
- Muslims believe that this life is a test from God which needs a judgement and rewards for those who pass, which can only happen if there is life after death.

Muslim beliefs about life after death affect the lives of Muslims because:

- the Last Day means only good Muslims will pass the judgement and go to paradise, so Muslims try to live good lives
- living a good Muslim life means observing the Five Pillars, which is why Muslims pray five times a day, fast during Ramadan, pay *zakah* and go on *hajj* at least once
- living a good Muslim life means following the Shari'ah, so they eat halal food, observe Muslim dress laws, do not drink alcohol, gamble or get involved in lending at interest
- belief in resurrection means that nothing should be removed from the body after death and funerals must take place within 48 hours.

Al'Jannah – heaven

Barzakh – the period between death and the Last Day

Israfil – the angel who begins the Last Day by blowing his trumpet

Jahannam – hell

Sources of wisdom and authority

- Surah 2 warns people to fear the Last Day when everyone will be treated as they deserve.
- Surah 9 says that heaven will be a beautiful garden through which rivers flow.
- Surah 4 says that hell will be a burning fire into which will be thrown those who reject God.
- Surah 4 says that people's only help on the Last Day will be the mercy and compassion of God.

Now test yourself

TESTED

1 *Al'Jannah* is:
  a) the period between death and the Last Day
  b) Arabic for heaven
  c) the angel who begins the Last Day by blowing his trumpet
  d) Arabic for hell

2 *Barzakh* is:
  a) the period between death and the Last Day
  b) Arabic for heaven
  c) the angel who begins the Last Day by blowing his trumpet
  d) Arabic for hell

3 Israfil is:
  a) the period between death and the Last Day
  b) Arabic for heaven
  c) the angel who begins the Last Day by blowing his trumpet
  d) Arabic for hell

4 *Jahannam* is:
  a) the period between death and the Last Day
  b) Arabic for heaven
  c) the angel who begins the Last Day by blowing his trumpet
  d) Arabic for hell

Activities

Complete the answers to these questions:

1 Outline three Muslim beliefs about the Last Day.

Muslims believe that when people die their body stays in the grave until the Last Day, Isa (Jesus) will return. A second belief is that the angel ....

A third belief is ....

2 Explain two different Muslim views about the final judgement. In your answer you must refer to a source of wisdom and authority.

Some Muslims believe that only good Muslims will pass God's judgement and enter paradise. They believe this because the Qur'an says that only those who have the right belief and who follow the religion and way of life taught by Muhammad will enter paradise.

However, many Muslims believe that God, 'the Merciful', 'the Compassionate', will forgive Muslims who have tried their best, because Surah 4 says that ....

Exam support

You need to know that the main religious tradition of Great Britain is Christianity. You also need to know about the similarities and differences between Muslim and Christian beliefs about life after death.

The table below might help you answer such questions.

Similarities	Differences
Both religions believe this life is not all there is and that there will be life after death.	Christians do not believe the dead need to be buried quickly.
Both believe there will be some form of judgement after death, based on how people have lived on earth.	Christians believe bodies can be cremated, while Muslims do not.
Both believe in heaven as a place of paradise with God.	Some Christians believe in immortality of the soul, but Muslims believe in resurrection of the body.
Both believe that good people will go to heaven.	Some Christians do not believe in the Last Day and believe judgement will take place as soon as people die.
Both believe that life after death is important because it makes sense of this life as it makes sure that the good are rewarded.	Catholic Christians believe that people who are not ready for heaven will go to purgatory to be cleansed of their sins before the Last Day.
	Some Christians do not believe in hell and believe that eventually everyone will go to heaven, while Muslims believe in hell.

2.2 Crime and punishment

Topic 2.2.1 Justice

REVISED

Justice means rewarding the good and punishing the bad, and making sure that what is right is what happens in society.

Why justice is important for Muslims

- The Qur'an describes God as just.
- The Qur'an says that God wants people to treat each other fairly and to establish justice.
- There are many **hadith** in which Muhammad is shown as acting justly and/or telling Muslims to treat everyone justly and equally.
- Equality before the law is one of the basic principles of the Islamic justice system. Justice has to be distributed with fairness, even if it goes against one's own self or one's parents or relatives and whether it goes against the rich or in favour of the poor.
- Muslims believe that all people should have equal rights before the law and that Muslims should work for a fairer sharing of the earth's resources. The pillar of *zakah* and the work of groups such as Muslim Aid and Islamic Relief all try to bring justice into the world.

Hadith – sayings of the Prophet Muhammad

Justice – due allocation of reward and punishment, the maintenance of right

Laws – rules made by Parliament and enforceable by the courts

Perpetrator – one who commits a crime

Victim – one who has suffered from a crime

Non-religious attitudes to justice

Justice is important for atheists and Humanists because a just society has **laws** which:

- ensure that people can work and be involved in business without someone taking away all the rewards of their work
- make sure that everyone behaves fairly to each other and that innocent people are protected from violence
- are upheld by courts and the police to ensure that all members of society obey the law.

Why justice is important for the victim

Victims of crime can suffer physically, financially and emotionally. Victims feel it is important that justice is done so that the hurt they have suffered is recognised by society and the **perpetrator** pays for their crime. Muslims believe that justice is important for the victim because:

- Islam teaches that justice should always be given and as the victim is totally innocent, justice can only be given when the victim receives justice.
- Islam teaches that the victims of crime should be compensated based on what is written in the Qur'an and making the criminal compensate their victim helps to give the victim justice.
- The fact that God commands Muslims to be just means that the unjust must be punished so that their victims are given justice.

Sources of wisdom and authority

- Surah 16 says that God commands justice and the doing of good from Muslims.
- Surah 49 says 'And act justly. Truly, God loves those who are just'.
- Surah 4 says that Muslims should stand up for justice even if it means acting against parents or relatives.

Now test yourself

TESTED

1 The due allocation of reward and punishment is called:
   a) law
   b) fairness
   c) justice
   d) jurisprudence
2 One who commits a crime is a:
   a) perpetrator
   b) victim
   c) hadith
   d) vicegerent
3 One who has suffered from a crime is a:
   a) perpetrator
   b) victim
   c) hadith
   d) vicegerent

Activities

Complete the answers to these questions:

1 Outline three ways in which crimes can hurt the victim.

Crimes such as theft can hurt a victim financially. It can hurt them emotionally if precious belongings are damaged. A third way it can hurt is .... physically – if someone is physically injured by a criminal.

2 Explain two reasons why justice is important for Muslims. In your answer you must refer to a source of wisdom and authority.

Justice is important for Muslims because they believe that it is part of their role as vicegerents of God's creation to behave justly to other people and to ensure that the world is governed in a fair way by following the Shari'ah. Islam has always had a system of justice based on courts with strict rules about how everyone should be treated fairly.

Surah 4 says that Muslims should ....

Exam support

You might be asked to evaluate a statement such as:

It is more important that the justice system protects society from crime than that it gives justice to the victims of crime.

The table below might help you answer such a question.

Arguments for	Arguments against
Protection from crime helps more people than giving justice to victims.	Islam teaches that justice should always be given and justice can only be given when the victim receives justice.
If society is not protected from crime, it will collapse and there will be chaos.	The Qur'an says that the victims of crime should be compensated, which helps to give them justice.
It is better to protect people from being hurt, than give them justice after they have been hurt.	The fact that God commands Muslims to be just means that the unjust must be punished so that their victims are given justice.
If the justice system protects society from crime successfully, there will be no victims of crime.	

Topic 2.2.2 Crime

REVISED

A crime is an act against the law, and laws are rules made about how members of society are expected to behave. The law is upheld by courts and the police to ensure that all members of society obey it.

Crime in the UK is classified as **acquisitive crime** (such as burglary), violent crime (ranging from minor assaults to murder) and **cybercrime** (crime committed on the internet).

The causes of crime

- Poverty is likely to lead people to crime. There is far more crime in poor areas than in rich areas and three-quarters of people convicted in 2008 had made a claim for out-of-work benefits.
- Upbringing and family background have a major effect on the likelihood of people committing crimes. People in prison are far more likely to have been in care, experienced abuse, been expelled from school or have family members who have been in prison, compared to the rest of the population.
- Alcohol and drugs are closely connected with crime. It has been suggested that between a third and a half of all acquisitive crime is related to illegal drug use. Drunkenness is associated with a majority of murders, manslaughters and stabbings.
- Sociological research shows a link between low **self-esteem** and criminal offending. Criminals in prison for drug offences and those with extensive criminal histories seem to have significantly lower self-esteem than the average.

Muslim attitudes to crime

- Islam tries to deal with the issue of poverty by banning interest in money lending (poverty is often made worse by high interest rates, which means some people become so desperate they turn to crime); encouraging Muslims to share their wealth; banning gambling which can drive people into poverty; using *zakah* to help poor Muslims in the UK; and encouraging Muslims to support policies aimed at removing poverty.
- Islam helps parents to fulfil their duties as Muslim parents. Muslim parents will be judged by God on how well they have brought up their children, so Muslim parents teach their children the difference between right and wrong and make sure they go to the ***madrasah***. Many mosques provide family advice and support if parents have problems.
- Alcohol and drugs should not be a problem for Muslim families because they are prohibited for Muslims (*haram*), being banned by the Qur'an and hadith.
- Muslims know they are the ***khalifahs*** of God and have been given the task of looking after the world in the way God wants, so they should never suffer from low self-esteem.

Islam tries to prevent criminals re-offending through:

- the Muslim Chaplains' Association which supports Muslim prison chaplains in their work of providing care in prisons and helping with the resettlement of prisoners and prevention of re-offending upon release
- the mentoring programme, Mosaic, which provides support to Muslim prisoners in the six months prior to their release from prison and for at least six months post-release to help them find employment and accommodation, and to help them with any problems they may have.

Acquisitive crime – crimes such as stealing and burglary where the criminal wants to acquire someone else's property

Cybercrime – criminal activities carried out by means of computers or the internet

Khalifahs – Allah's stewards or vicegerents

Madrasah – religious school or college

Self-esteem – a person's opinion of how good or important they are

Sources of wisdom and authority

- Surah 16 says that God commands justice, the doing of good and generosity.
- Surah 5 says that Muslims must have nothing to do with intoxicants (alcohol and drugs) and gambling.

Now test yourself

TESTED

1 Crimes such as stealing and burglary are examples of:
a) appropriate crime
b) acquisitive crime
c) cybercrime
d) analogue crime

2 Criminal activities carried out by means of computers or the internet are known as:
a) appropriate crime
b) acquisitive crime
c) cybercrime
d) analogue crime

3 Allah's stewards or vicegerents are called:
a) *Risalah*
b) *khalifahs*
c) *masjid*
d) *madrasah*

4 A Muslim religious school or college is a:
a) *Risalah*
b) *khalifahs*
c) *masjid*
d) *madrasah*

Activities

Complete the answers to these questions:

1 Outline three causes of crime.

Experts believe that poverty is a major cause of crime and studies show the majority of people in prison have been on benefits. Another cause of crime is upbringing, as children who have been in care or who come from a broken home are more likely to commit crimes. A third cause of crime is ....

....

2 Explain two ways in which Islam tries to remove the causes of crime. In your answer you must refer to a source of wisdom and authority.

Islam tries to remove poor upbringing as a cause of crime through its teachings on the family. Muslim parents are taught that they will be judged by God on how well they have brought up their children, so Muslim parents teach their children the difference between right and wrong and make sure they go to the madrasah. Many mosques provide family advice and support if parents have problems so that the children do not turn to crime.

Islam also tackles the problem of alcohol and drugs through its teachings. As Surah 5 says, ...

....

Exam support

You might be asked to evaluate a statement such as: *Religion could do a lot more to prevent crime.*

The table below might help you answer such a question.

Arguments for	Arguments against
Muslims make up a higher percentage of the prison population than the general population so more could be done to prevent this.	Islam tries to prevent people being driven to crime by poverty by banning interest, encouraging Muslims to share their wealth, banning gambling and using *zakah* to help poor Muslims.
Madrasahs could invite in the police to give talks on crime and its problems.	Islam encourages Muslim parents to bring their children up well by teaching that they will be judged by God on how well they have done this.
Mosques could give talks to parents on how to spot criminal activity in their children and how to prevent it.	The Qur'an and hadith ban Muslims from using alcohol and drugs, which are known to be factors in many crimes.
Muslims who have been in prison could be given opportunities to talk to their community about the problems crime causes and why Muslims need to avoid being sent to prison.	Islam gives Muslims a sense of self-worth because they know they are the *khalifahs* of God and have been given the task of looking after the world in the way God wants.

Topic 2.2.3 Muslim attitudes to good, evil and suffering

REVISED

The nature of good actions

All good actions are known as '*halal*' meaning 'that which is permitted' and Muslim scholars have subdivided good actions into two groups:

- ***Fard*** actions must be performed for a person to be regarded as good. They include obeying Shari'ah laws and observing the Five Pillars. Carrying out *fard* actions means a Muslim will be rewarded; not performing them will result in punishment.
- ***Mandub*** actions are those that Muslims will be rewarded for carrying out, but will not be punished for failing to carry out.

Islam teaches that those who perform good actions will be rewarded on the Day of Judgement by God sending them to paradise for eternity.

The nature of evil actions

Evil actions are called '***haram***', meaning 'that which is forbidden'. Any action which is forbidden in the Qur'an, the hadith or the Shari'ah, is *haram* and will be punished by God at the final judgement.

Non-religious attitudes to evil and suffering

Many non-religious people believe that evil and suffering exist because of the nature of the world. The suffering brought by things like diseases, floods and earthquakes (**natural evil**) are just part of how the world is. The evil brought by humans, such as crime and war (**moral evil**), is caused by humans being greedy, selfish and bigoted.

They believe that evil and suffering is a good reason for not believing in God because no good God would have created a world with diseases, floods, earthquakes, volcanoes, etc.

The Muslim answer to why people suffer

Evil and suffering causes a problem for Muslims because:

- if God is **omnipotent**, he must be able to remove evil and suffering from the world
- if God is **omnibenevolent**, he must want to remove evil and suffering from the world because they cause so much unhappiness.

Therefore, if God exists, there should be no evil or suffering in the world.

Muslims believe that God is omnipotent and omnibenevolent, so there must be a good reason for evil and suffering, but humans are not able to understand it. God is so much greater than humans that humans must just accept what God does. The Qur'an says Iblis defied God but he was allowed to try to tempt humans to choose wrong rather than right until the Day of Judgement.

Evil and suffering test people's belief in Islam and a true Muslim will remain faithful through the trials of this life, and be rewarded with eternity in paradise. The faithful should not ask why there is evil and suffering. Instead, they should accept it as God's will.

However, Islam also teaches that Muslims should try to remove evil and suffering from the world. Muslims respond to evil and suffering by helping those who suffer, either practically or by prayer, because helping the suffering and fighting evil will be rewarded by God on the Last Day.

Fard – actions which must be performed for a person to be regarded as good

Haram – that which is forbidden

Mandub – actions which a Muslim will be rewarded for doing, but will not be punished for not doing

Moral evil – actions done by humans which cause suffering.

Natural evil – things which cause suffering but have nothing to do with humans

Omnibenevolent – the belief that God is all-good

Omnipotent – the belief that God is all-powerful

Sources of wisdom and authority

- Surah 76 says that Muslims should accept what God sends with patience and constancy.
- Surah 67 tells Muslims that God is omnipotent, he has power over all things.
- 113 of the 114 surahs of the Qur'an begin by reminding Muslims that God is beneficent and merciful.

Now test yourself

TESTED

1 Actions which must be performed for a person to be regarded as good are:
   a) *haram*
   b) *fard*
   c) *mubah*
   d) *mandub*

2 Actions which a Muslim will be rewarded for doing, but will not be punished for not doing are:
   a) *haram*
   b) *fard*
   c) *mubah*
   d) *mandub*

3 Which of the following means that God is all-good?
   a) Omniscient
   b) Omnibenevolent
   c) Omnipotent
   d) Omnipresent

4 Which of the following means that God is all-powerful?
   a) Omniscient
   b) Omnibenevolent
   c) Omnipotent
   d) Omnipresent

Activities

Complete the answers to these questions:

1 Outline three Muslim beliefs about good actions.

All good actions are known as halal, meaning 'that which is permitted'. Another belief is that fard actions are ones that must be performed and Muslims will be punished for not performing them. A third belief is about mandub actions which ....

2 Explain two reasons why evil and suffering cause problems for Muslims. In your answer you must refer to a source of wisdom and authority.

Muslims believe that God is all-powerful. There are many surahs in the Qur'an which say that God has power over all things. This causes a problem because if God is all-powerful, he must be able to get rid of evil and suffering.

Muslims also believe that God is all-good. Of the 114 surahs of the Qur'an, 113 remind Muslims that God is ....

However, if God is beneficent and merciful, he must want to remove evil and suffering. So if God is both all-powerful and beneficent, there should be no evil and suffering in the world. The problem for Muslims is that there is.

Exam support

You might be asked to evaluate a statement such as:

Evil and suffering are not a problem if you believe in God/are a Muslim.

The table below might help you answer such a question.

Arguments for	Arguments against
There is a good reason for evil and suffering, but humans are not able to understand it because God is so much greater than humans.	If God is omnipotent, he must be able to remove evil and suffering from the world.
Evil and suffering test people's belief in Islam and a true Muslim will remain faithful through the trials of this life, and be rewarded with eternity in paradise.	If God is omnibenevolent, he must want to remove evil and suffering from the world because they cause so much unhappiness.
The faithful should not ask why there is evil and suffering. Instead, they should accept it as God's will.	It follows that, if God exists, there should be no evil or suffering in the world.
Helping the suffering and fighting evil will be rewarded by God on the Last Day.	As there is evil and suffering in the world, either God is not omnipotent, or God is not omni-benevolent, or God does not exist.

Topic 2.2.4 Attitudes to punishment

REVISED

The nature of punishment

Punishment is a penalty inflicted on an offender for breaking the law. Punishment can take many forms, but the main types imposed by UK courts are:

- imprisonment for a fixed period of time
- suspended sentence – the courts can impose imprisonment, but state that the order will not take effect for a fixed period of between one and three years unless the offender commits another offence within that time
- fine – a financial penalty; failure to pay will result in imprisonment
- community service order – an alternative to prison, this is unpaid work in the community; any breaches will result in imprisonment
- probation – offenders are placed under the supervision of a probation officer for a fixed period. If a probationer re-offends while on probation, or breaches the conditions of the probation order, they may be re-sentenced for the original offence.

Muslim teachings about punishment

Islam teaches that Muslims should not commit crimes because any crime is a sin against God. Those who commit crimes will not only be punished by the law, but will also face the judgement of God on the Last Day. Islam teaches that criminals should be punished for their crimes and the Qur'an sets down specific punishments for certain crimes, ranging from whipping to **amputation** to death. These are known as ***hadd* punishments** and are set for theft, wrong sexual relations (e.g. adultery), making unproven accusations, drinking intoxicants, apostasy (a Muslim denying Islam) and highway robbery. Strict requirements for evidence (including eyewitnesses) severely limit the application of the *hadd* penalties. The Qur'an also says that **compensation** can replace *hadd* punishments if both parties agree.

Most Muslims countries operate a legal and punishment system similar to those of Europe, and use ethical theories such as Situation Ethics to justify replacing the *hadd* punishments. Until recently, Saudi Arabia was the only country applying the *hadd* punishments, but now the Taleban, Daesh (Isis) and other areas under **Salafi** control tend to apply these punishments because they are set down in the Qur'an.

Punishment can be regarded as justice because when someone breaks the law, justice demands that they should be punished for what they have done. This is not revenge because it is not personal and it requires the punishment to be **proportional** to the crime, in other words the severity of the punishment must reflect the severity of the crime – for example, the death penalty for shoplifting would not be justice. Justice requires the good to be rewarded and the lawbreakers to be penalised and punishment is a way of doing this.

Punishment is needed in society because society needs people to obey the laws in order to operate efficiently – if there were no laws, or people could break the law without being punished, that would result in chaos. Punishment for those breaking the law ensures that society functions in an orderly way and benefits everyone, not just the strong.

Amputation – cutting off a limb

Compensation – paying back for a wrong done

***Hadd* punishments** – the punishments set down by the Qur'an

Proportional – the right level in relation to

Salafi – ultra-conservative reform movement in Sunni Islam

Sources of wisdom and authority

- Surah 5 says that the punishment for theft is cutting off the thief's hand as an example, from God, for their crime.
- Surah 42 says that punishment for an injury should be a similar injury, but compensation can replace this if the victim agrees to it.

Now test yourself

TESTED

1 Paying back for a wrong done is called:
   a) proportional
   b) retribution
   c) compensation
   d) probation
2 Punishment which is at the right level in relation to the crime committed is called:
   a) proportional
   b) retribution
   c) compensation
   d) probation
3 The punishments set down by the Qur'an are called:
   a) *fard*
   b) *haram*
   c) *hadd*
   d) *halal*
4 The ultra-conservative reform movement in Sunni Islam is called:
   a) Ismaili
   b) Salafi
   c) Sufi
   d) Sunni

Activities

Complete the answers to these questions:

1 Outline three types of punishment.

One type of punishment is imprisonment for a fixed period of time. Another type is a fine, which is a financial penalty; failure to pay will result in imprisonment. A third type of punishment is ....

....

2 Explain two reasons why punishment is important for Muslims. In your answer you must refer to a source of wisdom and authority.

Punishment is important for Muslims because Islam teaches that criminals should be punished for their crimes. Islam teaches that Muslims should not commit crimes because any crime is a sin against God. Therefore, those who commit crimes will not only be punished by the law, but they will also face the judgement of God on the Last Day.

Another reason is that the Qur'an sets down specific punishments for particular crimes – these range from whipping to amputation to death. Surah 5 says that the punishment for theft is ....

....

Exam support

You might be asked to evaluate a statement such as:

Punishment is better dealt with by the state than by religion.

The table below might help you answer such a question.

Arguments for	Arguments against
The state can deal with criminals whatever their religion, whereas a religion can only deal with those who believe it.	Criminals are more likely to be changed by punishment if they believe it comes from God.
The state can adjust its punishments as society and crimes change over time, but religion has to continue to follow its holy book.	The punishments of Islam are set out in the Qur'an, which Muslims believe comes directly from God, so the punishments must come directly from God.
The state can take into account the findings of research about which punishments work best.	God knows better than the state as to what punishments will work, because God is all-knowing and all-wise.
The state has the money to ensure that punishments are properly funded.	The state can be corrupted and may let rich, powerful criminals avoid punishment, whereas religion will be applied equally no matter what a person's personal circumstances.

Topic 2.2.5 The aims of punishment

REVISED

The aims of punishment

Punishment aims to:

- make sure that everyone obeys the law
- protect law-abiding members of society from the law breakers
- deter law-abiding citizens from committing crimes
- reform and rehabilitate criminals so that they do not break the law in the future
- penalise criminals for their actions and give the victims of crime a sense of retribution.

There are various theories about what type of punishment works best:

- **Retribution** – this is the theory that criminals should pay for their crime. Some people think this is the best type of punishment because it makes criminals suffer for what they have done wrong. Criminals make their victims suffer, so the criminals should also suffer.
- **Deterrence** – this is the theory that the punishment should put people off committing crime. Some people think this is the best type of punishment because if the punishment is severe enough, no one will dare to commit the crime. For example, if a person knows they will have their hand cut off if they are caught stealing, they will not steal.
- **Reform** – this is the theory that criminals should be taught not to commit crimes again. Some people think this is the best form of punishment because the only way to stop crime is to reform the criminal so that they become law-abiding citizens who will not want to commit crimes again.
- **Protection** – this is the theory that punishment should protect society from criminals and their activities. Some people think this is the best form of punishment because if murderers and terrorists are executed, they cannot threaten people; if violent people or persistent burglars are given long prison sentences, people and their property are protected.

Deterre nce – the theory that punishments should be harsh to discourage people from commiting crime

Ordinance – a law

Protection – the theory that punishments should protect society from criminals

Reform – the theory that punishment should try to change criminals into law-abiding citizens

Retribution – the theory that criminals should be punished for what they have done

Muslim attitudes to the aims of punishment

The *hadd* punishments are based on retribution, deterrence and reform. It is believed that fear of these types of punishment will deter most people from committing crimes. They also make the criminal pay for their crime (retribution) and will reform the criminal because a thief who has had one hand cut off will never steal again in case they get the other hand cut off.

Surah 4 of the Qur'an says 'God doth wish to make clear to you and to show you the **ordinances** of those before you and He doth wish to you in mercy'.

Imprisonment is also used in Muslim countries to protect society from anti-social criminals.

Many Muslims countries believe that the aims of punishment (protection, retribution, deterrence and reform) are best achieved by such punishments as imprisonment because the *hadd* punishments are no longer relevant and have never been compulsory in Islam.

Most Muslims believe that criminals should be fairly treated and that punishment should aim at both reforming criminals and bringing about restorative justice.

Sources of wisdom and authority

- Surah 4 suggests that Muslims should be merciful in their punishments.
- Surah 5 says that the punishment for theft is cutting off the thief's hand.

Now test yourself

TESTED

1 The theory that criminals should be punished for what they have done is:
a) ordinance
b) deterrence
c) reformation
d) retribution

2 The theory that punishment should try to change criminals into law-abiding citizens is:
a) ordinance
b) deterrence
c) reform
d) retribution

3 Another name for a law is:
a) ordinance
b) deterrence
c) reform
d) retribution

4 The theory that punishments should be so harsh no one would dare commit a crime is:
a) ordinance
b) deterrence
c) reform
d) retribution

Activities

Complete the answers to these questions:

1 Outline three aims of punishment.

One aim of punishment is retribution – the idea that criminals should be punished for what they have done. Another aim is deterrence – the theory that punishments should be harsh to discourage people from committing crimes. A third aim is ....

2 Explain Muslim attitudes to the aims of punishment. In your answer you must refer to a source of wisdom and authority.

Muslims believe that punishment should be based on retribution, deterrence and reform. The theory is that the hadd punishments set out in the Qur'an will deter most people from committing crimes because they will be frightened of the punishment. They also make the criminal pay for their crime (retribution) and will reform the criminal because, for example, a thief who has had one hand cut off will never steal again in case they get the other hand cut off.

This attitude is based on such Qur'anic teachings such as Surah 5, which says that ....

....

Exam support

You might be asked to evaluate a statement such as:

Religious people should be concerned with reforming criminals, not punishing them.

The table below might help you answer such a question.

Arguments for	Arguments against
The evidence seems to be that punishment does not stop people committing crimes, because around half of those sent to prison re-offend within a year of their release.	The Qur'an teaches that those who break the law should be punished.
Islam is based on the idea of God's mercy to sinners and giving them a chance to change their ways.	Surah 5 says: 'As to the thief, male or female, cut off his or her hands: a punishment by way of example, from God, for their crime'.
'God doth wish to make clear to you and to show you the ordinances of those before you and He doth wish to you in mercy'.	Justice requires the good to be rewarded and the lawbreakers penalised – punishment is a way of doing this.

Topic 2.2.6 Forgiveness

REVISED

Muslim beliefs about forgiveness

The Qur'an teaches that God is compassionate and merciful to sinners because:

- On the Day of Judgement, God will deal with everyone as they deserve, but Muslims will be able to request his mercy. However, how can Muslims ask for God's forgiveness if they are not prepared to forgive?
- The Qur'an says that Muslims should forgive other people's sins against them.
- There are many hadith from the Prophet Muhammad about forgiving people who have offended others and bringing reconciliation to conflicts.

Why offenders need to be forgiven by the community

The prison system costs British taxpayers £11bn each year and up to 60 per cent of prisoners reoffend. The community needs to forgive offenders and help them to **reintegrate** into law-abiding society so that they are part of society and will not need to return to a life of crime.

How offenders are forgiven by the community

- The UK government tries to **rehabilitate** offenders through the Rehabilitation of Offenders Act 1974 (amended 2012).
- Some business owners are helping to bring offenders back into the community by offering them employment and training. For example, The Joint is a restaurant in Brixton that provides jobs for those trained at Gordon Ramsay's Bad Boys' Bakery at Brixton prison.
- A large number of charities work to help ex-offenders to become law-abiding members of society, for example Nacro, which offers information and advice to ex-offenders, their families and friends.

Rehabilitation – restoring to normal, productive life

Reintegrate – to fit someone back into society

Restorative justice – a system of criminal justice which focuses on the rehabilitation of offenders through reconciliation with victims and the community

Restorative justice

Restorative justice gives victims of crime the chance to explain to the offender how they have been affected by a crime and to ask any questions they may have about the incident. Offenders thus have the chance to understand the impact of their crime and take action to repair the harm caused. One of the obvious benefits of restorative justice is the extremely high levels of satisfaction among victims who take part. Eighty per cent of offenders also said that restorative justice had helped them by making them realise the effects of their crime and giving them the determination to turn their backs on crime.

Muslims are in favour of restorative justice because it is the only way of bringing peace and reconciliation between the criminal and the victim, which is what the Qur'an encourages. In Islam, all Muslims are brothers and sisters and should work to help each other. The Qur'an also says that on the Last Day those who have not been brought face to face with the evil they have done and repented of it will be punished.

Sources of wisdom and authority

- Surah 39 suggests that Muslims should never despair of God's mercy because God is the 'Oft-Forgiving, Most Merciful'.
- In a hadith, Muhammad said that Muslims should be forgiving and give justice to the person who was unfair and unjust to them.

Now test yourself

TESTED

1 *Bismillah* refers to:
   a) the belief in God's forgiveness
   b) the closing words of *salah*
   c) the words which begin the surahs
   d) the belief in God's oneness
2 Legal accountability means:
   a) paying taxes to support the legal system
   b) being responsible before the law for your actions
   c) restoring to normal, productive life
   d) punishment which focuses on reconciling offenders with their victims and the community
3 Rehabilitation means:
   a) paying taxes to support the legal system
   b) being responsible before the law for your actions
   c) restoring to normal, productive life
   d) punishment which focuses on reconciling offenders with their victims and the community
4 Restorative justice means:
   a) paying taxes to support the legal system
   b) being responsible before the law for your actions
   c) restoring to normal, productive life
   d) punishment which focuses on reconciling offenders with their victims and the community

Activities

Complete the answers to these questions:

1 Outline three examples of how society forgives criminals.

The UK government shows forgiveness by helping offenders through the Rehabilitation of Offenders Act. Some business owners show forgiveness by helping to rehabilitate offenders by giving them work opportunities and training.

Another example is ....

2 Explain two reasons why forgiveness is important for Muslims. In your answer you must refer to a source of wisdom and authority.

Forgiveness is important for Muslims because on the Day of Judgement God will deal with everyone as they deserve, but Muslims will be able to request his mercy. Muslims must be prepared to forgive others, however, if they wish to ask for God's forgiveness for themselves. Another reason is that the Qur'an says that Muslims should forgive other people's sins against them and Muslims should obey the Qur'an as they believe it is the word of God.

Muhammad said in a hadith that Muslims should ....

Exam support

You might be asked to evaluate a statement such as:

Criminals are more likely to be forgiven and reintegrated into society by religious people.

The table below might help you answer such a question.

Arguments for	Arguments against
On the Day of Judgement God will deal with everyone as they deserve, which means Muslims need to forgive others if they are to be forgiven by God.	Societies using the *hadd* punishments fixed in the Qur'an do not reintegrate people who have had a hand amputated for theft, for example.
The Qur'an says that Muslims should forgive other people's sins against them and Muslims should obey the Qur'an as they believe it is the word of God.	Religious societies seem to have more severe punishments than those that are not religious.
There are many hadith from the Prophet Muhammad about forgiving people who have offended others and bringing reconciliation to conflicts, and Muslims believe they should follow the example of the Prophet.	Restorative justice has been introduced in societies not based on religion.

Topic 2.2.7 The treatment of criminals

REVISED

Human rights

All the member states of the United Nations agreed to the Universal Declaration of Human Rights in 1948, which sets out a number of human rights which must be protected. With regard to crime and punishment, this protects, among other things, an individual's right to:

- freedom of thought, conscience and religion
- **freedom of expression**
- a fair trial
- legal representation at their trial
- **humane** treatment while in custody
- not be subjected to torture
- punishment that is proportionate to the crime
- not be treated as an adult, if the individual is a juvenile.

Muslim attitudes to the treatment of criminals

- Islamic states which have adopted Western-type legal systems provide fair trials where the accused is tried in open court with a defence lawyer (**legal representation**) and a jury of twelve ordinary citizens who decide whether the defendant is guilty. The judge makes sure that that the case is conducted fairly and decides what punishment should be given if the defendant is found guilty.
- However, Muslim countries operating Shari'ah legal systems do not use juries or prosecutors and sometimes not even defence lawyers. Crimes against God (including drinking alcohol, lending at interest and committing adultery) are prosecuted by the state as ***hudud* crimes**. All other criminal matters, including murder and bodily injury, are treated as disputes between individuals, with an Islamic judge deciding the outcome based on the Shari'ah.
- Most Muslims are opposed to the use of torture as the Prophet Muhammad issued several hadith condemning its use. The vast majority of Muslim countries have signed the United Nations Convention Against Torture which commits them to preventing acts of torture in their territory.
- However, some Muslims believe it is permitted to torture criminals in certain circumstances and would use ethical theories such as Situation Ethics or Utilitarianism, where the greatest good for the greatest number of people would justify using torture in certain situations (for example, if someone has planted a bomb in a school, it would be right to torture them so that they identify the school and it can be evacuated).
- Many Muslims agree with the Universal Declaration of Human Rights and make sure that human rights are always respected.
- Many Muslims believe that human rights are subject to Islamic Shari'ah and the teachings of the Qur'an, which means that in Muslim countries there are often no gay rights, no right of **consensual sex** outside of marriage, no freedom of religion and no equal rights for women.

Consensual sex – sex to which both parties freely agree

Freedom of expression – the freedom to express your opinions in public (especially about politics and religion)

***Hudud* crimes** – crimes against God

Humane – treating with kindness and compassion

Legal representation – a lawyer who makes sure their client is treated fairly and has their case put to best effect

Sources of wisdom and authority

- Muhammad said in a hadith that God will torture those who torture other people.
- Surah 5 says that the punishment for those who act against Islam is execution, or crucifixion, or the cutting off of hands and feet from opposite sides.

Now test yourself

TESTED

1 Which of these is *not* a crime against God?
   a) Drinking alcohol
   b) Lending at interest
   c) Eating meat
   d) Committing adultery
2 Which of these is *not* a human right?
   a) The right to a fair trial
   b) The right to freedom of expression
   c) The right to a fair wage
   d) The right to freedom of religion
3 Crimes against God are called:
   a) *hadd* crimes
   b) *hudud* crimes
   c) *haram* crimes
   d) *hadith* crimes
4 Which of the following is *not* required for a trial to be considered 'fair'?
   a) A legal representative for the defendant
   b) To be held in open court
   c) An independent judge
   d) Muslim lawyers

Activities

Complete the answers to these questions:

1 Outline three human rights criminals should have under the Universal Declaration of Human Rights.

The UN Declaration says that criminals should have a right to be treated humanely while in custody. It says that torture must never be used. It also says that ....

2 Explain two different Muslim attitudes to the treatment of criminals. In your answer you must refer to a source of wisdom and authority.

Most Muslims believe that criminals should be fairly treated and that punishment should aim to reform criminals and bring about restorative justice. Both the Muslim Prison Chaplains Association and Muslim Aid work with Muslim prisoners to achieve these ends.

However, Muslims who believe in Shari'ah justice systems believe that criminals should be punished according to the hadd punishments set out in the Qur'an, such as Surah 5 which says ....

....

Exam support

You might be asked to evaluate a statement such as: *Religion ensures the best treatment of criminals.*

The table below might help you answer such a question.

Arguments for	Arguments against
Most Muslims believe that criminals should be fairly treated.	Muslim countries operating Shari'ah law do not always allow criminals legal representation.
Most Muslims believe that the aim of punishment should be to reform criminals and help them to live an honest life on their release.	Shari'ah law does not permit trial by jury.
Both the Muslim Prison Chaplains Association and Muslim Aid work with Muslim prisoners while they are serving their sentences and support them when they are released.	Shari'ah law uses *hadd* punishments which infringe human rights as well as punishing some criminals by flogging, which non-Muslims regard as torture.
Most Muslims are opposed to the use of torture.	

Topic 2.2.8 The death penalty

REVISED

Capital punishment (the **death penalty**) is punishment which takes away the criminal's life. A crime which can be punished by the death penalty is called a **capital offence**. There are several methods of capital punishment still in use around the world, including **lethal injection**, the electric chair, hanging and death by firing squad.

Only 37 of the world's 195 countries use capital punishment; the USA, Japan and Singapore are the only industrialised countries to retain it. The United Kingdom abolished the death penalty in 1970.

People who believe in capital punishment believe it deters people from committing murder, protects society and gives retribution to those who take life.

Muslim attitudes to capital punishment

Islam allows capital punishment for three offences: murder, adultery and **apostasy**. Most Muslims agree with capital punishment because:

- it is a punishment set down by God in the Qur'an and Muslims believe the Qur'an is the word of God
- Muhammad made several statements agreeing with capital punishment for murder, adultery and apostasy
- Muhammad sentenced people to death for murder when he was ruler of Madinah.

Some Muslims do not agree with capital punishment because:

- they feel that capital punishment is recommended by the Qur'an, but is not compulsory
- the Shari'ah says that the family of a murder victim can accept blood money from the murderer, rather than requiring the death sentence
- they feel that capital punishment does not reduce crime
- there is a possibility of the wrong person being convicted and then executed, which would mean capital punishment is not justice and so is banned by Surah 6:151.

Apostasy – giving up or denying your religious faith

Capital offence – a crime which can be punished by death

Death penalty – death as the punishment for a crime

Indeterminate life sentence – being imprisoned for the rest of one's life, with no chance of ever being released

Lethal injection – executing a criminal by injecting them with sufficient poison to kill them

Non-religious attitudes to capital punishment

Humanists are against capital punishment because of ethical theories such as Situation Ethics or Utilitarianism:

- Sometimes people are convicted for offences which it is later proved they did not commit. Those who are found to be innocent can be released and compensated if they have been given life imprisonment, but not if they have been executed.
- Statistics show that those countries which do not use the death penalty have a lower murder rate, so capital punishment does not deter people from committing such an offence.
- Human life is the most important thing and no one has the right to take it. Executing murderers demonstrates that society does not regard human life as sacred.
- Murderers often regard an **indeterminate life sentence** as worse than death and many try to commit suicide when in prison for life.

Some atheists agree with the Humanist attitude to capital punishment, while others support the death penalty because they believe:

- The prospect of losing your life if you commit murder acts as a deterrent.
- The value of human life can only be demonstrated by inflicting the worst penalty on those who take life, which is the death penalty.

Sources of wisdom and authority

- Various Qur'anic verses recommend execution as a punishment for serious crimes.
- Surah 5 says that the punishment for those who act against Islam is execution, or crucifixion, or the cutting off of hands and feet from opposite sides.
- In a well-recorded hadith, Muhammad says that Muslims can only be executed for adultery, murder or deserting the faith.

Now test yourself

TESTED

1 Apostasy is:
   a) a crime which can be punished by death
   b) death as the punishment for a crime
   c) a Muslim giving up and working against his religious faith
   d) executing a criminal by injecting them with sufficient poison to kill them
2 A capital offence is:
   a) a crime which can be punished by death
   b) death as the punishment for a crime
   c) a Muslim giving up and working against his religious faith
   d) executing a criminal by injecting them with sufficient poison to kill them
3 The death penalty is:
   a) a crime which can be punished by death
   b) death as the punishment for a crime
   c) a Muslim giving up and working against his religious faith
   d) executing a criminal by injecting them with sufficient poison to kill them
4 The family of a murder victim can accept blood money from the murderer rather than requiring the death sentence, according to:
   a) the hadith
   b) the Shari'ah
   c) the *ummah*
   d) the *shahadah*

Activities

Complete the answers to these questions:

1 Outline three reasons why Humanists are against capital punishment.

Humanists are against capital punishment because people are sometimes convicted for offences which it is later proved they did not commit and nothing can be done if they have been executed. Also statistics show that those countries which do not use the death penalty have a lower murder rate. A third reason is ....

....

2 Explain two reasons why Muslims believe in capital punishment. In your answer you must refer to a source of wisdom and authority.

Muslims believe in capital punishment because Muhammad made several statements agreeing with capital punishment for murder, adultery and apostasy. Muslims believe that Muhammad is the seal of the prophets whose words should be obeyed.

Another reason is that the death penalty is a punishment set down in the Qur'an. Indeed Surah 5 says that..

Exam support

You might be asked to evaluate a statement such as: *Death is the best punishment for murderers.*

The table below might help you answer such a question.

Arguments for	Arguments against
Death is a punishment set down by God in the Qur'an, so it is divine punishment.	Sometimes people are convicted for offences which it is later proved they did not commit. Innocent people cannot be released and compensated if they have been executed.
Muhammad made several statements agreeing with capital punishment for murder, adultery and apostasy and so it is recommended by the seal of the prophets.	Statistics show that those countries which do not use the death penalty have a lower murder rate, so capital punishment is not an effective deterrent.
Muhammad sentenced people to death for murder when he was ruler of Madinah and so it must be the best punishment.	Human life is the most important thing and so no one has the right to take it.
The Shari'ah says that capital punishment is the punishment for murder, adultery and apostasy, and the Shari'ah is the holy law of Islam.	Murderers often regard life imprisonment as worse than death and try to commit suicide when in prison.

2.3 Living the Muslim life

Topic 2.3.1 The Ten Obligatory Acts

REVISED

For Sunni Muslims, performing the Five Pillars (***shahadah***, ***salah***, ***zakah***, ***sawm*** and ***hajj***) is the practical expression of being a Muslim and observing all five shows that a Muslim is a good Muslim. However, Shi'a Islam teaches that there are Ten Obligatory Acts a Muslim must perform to show that they are good Shi'a Muslims:

1. *Salah* – the ritual prayer performed at set times, five times a day (there are some slight differences between the Sunni *salah* and the Shi'a *salah*).
2. *Sawm* – fasting during the month of **Ramadan**.
3. *Zakah* – the obligatory charity tax.
4. *Hajj* – the annual pilgrimage to Makkah.
5. ***Khums*** – a special type of *zakah* where a fifth of certain types of income must go to charity.
6. *Jihad* – the struggle to be a good Muslim.
7. *Amr-bil-ma'ruf* – always doing that which is good.
8. *Nahi anil munkar* – always avoiding that which is evil.
9. ***Tawalla*** – loving the relatives of the Prophet; this is closely connected with the Shi'a belief in the Imams and those who can trace their ancestry back to Muhammad receive special treatment from Shi'a Muslims.
10. *Tabarra* – hating those who hate Allah and his chosen ones.

The Obligatory Acts are based on a reference in Surah 9, but were developed by the Twelve Imams (all of whom were descendants of the Prophet Muhammad). The Acts were probably developed to differentiate Shi'a Muslims from the Sunnis.

The Ten Obligatory Acts are important for Shi'as because:

- they were established by Muhammad, Ali and the Imams
- Allah will punish those who do not fulfil the Acts
- by fulfilling the Acts Shi'a Muslims can have confidence that on the Day of Judgement, Allah will allow them into heaven
- the Obligatory Acts are a major way of differentiating Shi'a from Sunni Muslims.

Sunni Muslims and their relationship with the Five Pillars

The four practical pillars (*salah*, *sawm*, *zakah* and *hajj*) are part of the Acts, and it is likely that they were developed before Sunni Muslims had accepted the *shahadah* as the first pillar. This is why *shahadah* is not one of the Ten Obligatory Acts, but is regarded by Shi'as as essential for becoming a Muslim (though the Shi'a *shahadah* adds a reference to Imam Ali).

The last six Acts are not in the Five Pillars, but Sunnis believe that doing that which is good and avoiding evil are essential features of being a Muslim, and many Sunnis regard *jihad* as the sixth pillar. However, Sunnis regard the last two Acts as totally wrong and against Islam because Sunnis believe Muhammad's relatives and descendants have no particular authority or importance.

Hajj – pilgrimage to Makkah, the fifth pillar

Khums – an additional charity tax for Shi'a Muslims

Ramadan – ninth month of the Islamic year; the month of fasting

Salah – ritual prayers to be said five times a day, the second pillar

Sawm – fasting, the fourth pillar

Shahadah – the confession and witness of faith, the first pillar

Tawalla – loving the relatives of the Prophet

Zakah – charity tax, the third pillar

Sources of wisdom and authority

- Surah 5 says that those who do good and forbid what is wrong will gain paradise.
- Surah 9 says that true believers are protectors of one another, do what is just and forbid what is evil and observe regular prayers and practise regular charity.

Now test yourself

TESTED

1 Loving the relatives of the Prophet is called:
   a) *khums*
   b) *salah*
   c) *tawalla*
   d) *sawm*
2 An additional charity tax for Shi'a Muslims is called:
   a) *khums*
   b) *salah*
   c) *tawalla*
   d) *sawm*
3 Ritual prayers to be said five times a day (the second pillar) are called:
   a) *khums*
   b) *salah*
   c) *tawalla*
   d) *sawm*
4 Fasting (the fourth pillar) is called:
   a) *khums*
   b) *salah*
   c) *tawalla*
   d) *sawm*

Activities

Complete the answers to these questions:

1 Outline three of the Ten Obligatory Acts of Shi'a Islam.

The Ten Obligatory Acts are what a Shi'a Muslim should do to show they are a good Shi'a. One of the Acts is hajj which means going on pilgrimage to Makkah. Another is paying the charity tax of zakah. A third Obligatory Act is ....

2 Explain two reasons why the Ten Obligatory Acts are important for Shi'a Muslims. In your answer you must refer to a source of wisdom and authority.

The Ten Obligatory Acts are important because they were established by Muhammad and the Imams, the founders of Shi'a Islam. The Acts are also important because they differentiate the Shi'a from Sunni Muslims and are referred to in the Qur'an the holy book of Islam.

Surah 9 says that true believers ....

Exam support

You might be asked to evaluate a statement such as:

The Ten Obligatory Acts should be performed by all Muslims.

The table below might help you answer such a question.

Arguments for	Arguments against
They incorporate the four practical pillars which all Muslims should perform.	Sunni Muslims will not obey the Ten Acts because loving the relatives of the Prophet contradicts the view that Muhammad is the final prophet.
All Muslims should obey the Qur'an and Surah 9:71 says doing good and avoiding evil is necessary for all Muslims.	Sunni Muslims believe that hating those who hate Allah's chosen ones refers to the Imams, who Sunni Muslims believe have betrayed Islam, and so should be hated.
Khums is very similar to the Sunni *sadaqah* so there is no reason why all Muslims should not follow it.	*Khums* is not a pillar and Sunnis believe it is not a compulsory tax; only *zakah* is compulsory for them.
All Muslims should love the relatives of the Prophet and hate those who hate Allah and his chosen ones.	The Ten Obligatory Acts make no mention of the *shahadah* which is the first pillar for Sunni Muslims.

Topic 2.3.2 *Shahadah*

REVISED

What is the *shahadah*?

Shahadah means 'to observe, witness, testify' and the Shahadah says 'bear witness that there is no god but God and that Muhammad is the prophet of God'.

These simple beliefs sum up Islam: If you believe in God's unity then you believe in the unity of creation and humanity, the **vicegerency** of humans, angels, prophets and holy books. If you believe that Muhammad is the Prophet of God, then you accept the Qur'an as the word of God and the Sunnah of Muhammad as the path to follow in your life.

Some scholars believe that, although it is now the first pillar, *shahadah* was originally the last of the pillars because the four active pillars are commanded in the Qur'an, but the *shahadah* simply sums up the beliefs of Islam. The active pillars are ways of ***ibadah*** (worship), but you cannot worship without the faith (***iman***) on which the worship is based. The *shahadah* acts as the creed of Islam and is a sign that the person reciting is a Muslim.

Ibadah – worship

Iman – faith

Minaret – the tower beside the mosque from which the call to prayer is announced

Muezzin – the prayer caller who announces the call to prayer five times a day

Polytheism – worshipping many gods

Vicegerency – looking after something on behalf of someone else

The importance of *shahadah* for Muslims today

The *shadadah* is important because:

- it is the creed of Islam which sums up the faith
- there are no ceremonies such as baptism or Bar Mitzvah to make you a Muslim and so the *shahadah* is of crucial importance because if someone converts, they have to recite the *shahadah* in front of Muslim witnesses to become a Muslim
- it shows that Muslims reject **polytheism** – there is no god but God
- it shows that Islam rejects Christian beliefs about Jesus being the Son of God – Muhammad is nothing more than a prophet
- the *shahadah* is called from the **minaret** of the mosque by the **muezzin** five times a day
- good Muslims recite the *shahadah* at least five times a day in their *salah* prayers.

The *shahadah* in Shi'a Islam

The Shi'a also teach that reciting the *shahadah* in Arabic is all that is required for a person to become a Muslim. However:

- Most Shi'a add 'Ali is the vicegerent of God' at the end of the *shahadah* to show their belief that Ali is the leader of the believers, along with God and Muhammad.
- *Shahadah* is not one of the Obligatory Acts for Shi'as, whereas it is the first pillar for Sunnis.

Sources of wisdom and authority

- Surah 3 says that Islam's basic belief is that 'There is no god but He, the Exalted in Power'.
- Muslim scholars have declared that *shahadah* 'is the central pillar even though it is the only "non-action" pillar.'

Now test yourself

TESTED

1 Muezzin is:
   a) the Muslim word for worship
   b) the Muslim word for faith
   c) the tower beside the mosque from which the call to prayer is announced
   d) the prayer caller who announces the call to prayer five times a day

2 *Ibadah* is:
   a) the Muslim word for worship
   b) the Muslim word for faith
   c) the tower beside the mosque from which the call to prayer is announced
   d) the prayer caller who announces the call to prayer five times a day

3 *Iman* is:
   a) the Muslim word for worship
   b) the Muslim word for faith
   c) the tower beside the mosque from which the call to prayer is announced
   d) the prayer caller who announces the call to prayer five times a day

4 Minaret is:
   a) the Muslim word for worship
   b) the Muslim word for faith
   c) the tower beside the mosque from which the call to prayer is announced
   d) the prayer caller who announces the call to prayer five times a day

Activities

Complete the answers to these questions:

1 Outline three of the active pillars.

Salah is an active pillar as Muslims have to perform the actions and pray to Allah five times a day. Zakah is an active pillar because Muslims have to pay the tax. Another active pillar is ....

....

2 Explain two reasons why *shahadah* is important for Muslims today. In your answer you must refer to a source of wisdom and authority.

The shahadah is of crucial importance for Muslims because if someone converts to Isam, all they have to do is recite the shahadah in front of Muslim witnesses and then they are a Muslim. Another reason is that the shahadah is the creed of Islam, which sums up the faith and shows that Muslims reject polytheism. Surah 3 says that ....

Exam support

You might be asked to evaluate a statement such as:

The shahadah *is the most important of the Five Pillars.*

The table below might help you answer such a question.

Arguments for	Arguments against
The *shahadah* is the Muslim creed which sums up the faith.	*Salah* is more important because the *shahadah* is repeated several times as a part of *salah*.
If someone converts to Islam, they must recite the *shahadah* in front of Muslim witnesses in order to become a Muslim.	*Salah* puts Muslims in direct contact with God five times a day.
The *shahadah* shows that Muslims reject polytheism – there is no god but God.	*Salah* reminds Muslims every day that they have submitted themselves to God.
The *shahadah* shows that Islam rejects Christian beliefs about Jesus being the Son of God – Muhammad is nothing more than a prophet.	*Salah* unites worshippers with their fellow Muslims and reminds them of the unity of Islam as they stand in lines performing the same actions.

Topic 2.3.3 *Salah*

REVISED

The history of *salah*

Muhammad began a system of morning and evening prayers during which people faced Jerusalem and **prostrated** themselves to show their submission to God. When Muhammad established the Muslim community in Madinah in 622CE, the direction of prayer was changed to Makkah.

To prepare for prayer, Muslim do the following:

- Remove their shoes.
- Perform ***wudu*** (washing hands, arms to the elbow, face, nostrils, ears and head, and washing the feet three times in running water). This is so a Muslim is as pure as possible before the sacred moment of *salah* when they make direct contact with God.
- Find a clean place.
- Face the direction of Makkah (*qibla*).

The prayer ritual is called a ***raka*** and each prayer time has a set number of *rakat* during which the worshippers do the following:

- Recite Surah 1.
- Prostrate themselves several times, giving glory to God.
- Repeat the *shahadah*.
- Request God's blessing on the people around them and for Muhammad and all the prophets.

Salah must be said in Arabic, with all the people praying performing the same actions and facing the same direction.

Some Muslims say their prayers at home as a family in a special clean room with prayer mats which are kept facing Makkah.

Others think it is preferable to pray in the mosque and all mosques have communal *wudu* facilities and a prayer hall whose carpet has lines directed to the prayer wall where the ***mihrab*** (***qibla*** alcove) indicates the direction of the Ka'aba. The worshippers stand in lines behind the **imam** (prayer leader) who leads them through the ritual. Most mosques have a special area for women to perform *salah*.

Jummah prayers

The Qur'an commands Muslims to say their midday prayers on a Friday in a mosque. These are called **jummah** prayers. During them, the imam preaches a sermon (***khutba***), often giving advice on how to live a good Muslim life in the country they are in. Muslims living in a non-Muslim country would need an hour or so off work on Friday to attend *jummah* prayers and be good Muslims.

Why *salah* is important to Muslims today

- It puts them in direct contact with God five times a day.
- It reminds them every day that they have submitted themselves to God.
- It unites them with their fellow Muslims as they stand in lines performing the same actions and saying the same words.
- It is a discipline which forces Muslims to take their religion seriously.
- It is a way of having sins forgiven because a hadith says: 'the five prayers remove sins as water removes dirt'.

Imam – prayer leader

Jummah – Friday midday prayers

Khutba – sermon

Mihrab – alcove in mosques showing direction of Makkah

Prostrated – to put oneself flat on the ground so as to be lying face downwards, especially in submission

Qibla – direction of the Ka'aba in Makkah

Raka – the set actions in the prayer ritual (plural *rakat*)

Wudu – the ritual washing before prayers

Sources of wisdom and authority

- Surah 4 says that Muslims must make regular prayers at the set times.
- Surah 2 says that Muslims must make their prayers facing in the direction of the Sacred Mosque.
- Surah 5 says that Muslims must wash their faces and hands to the elbows, and rub their heads and feet up to the ankles before they pray.
- Surah 62 says that Muslims must leave work when the call to prayer is made on Friday, but when the prayer is finished, they can go back to work.

Now test yourself

TESTED

1 *Jummah* refers to:
  a) Friday midday prayers
  b) a Muslim sermon
  c) the direction of the Ka'aba in Makkah
  d) the ritual washing before prayers
2 *Wudu* is:
  a) Friday midday prayers
  b) a Muslim sermon
  c) the direction of the Ka'aba in Makkah
  d) the ritual washing before prayers
3 *Qibla* is:
  a) Friday midday prayers
  b) a Muslim sermon
  c) the direction of the Ka'aba in Makkah
  d) the ritual washing before prayers
4 *Khutba* is:
  a) Friday midday prayers
  b) a Muslim sermon
  c) the direction of the Ka'aba in Makkah
  d) the ritual washing before prayers

Activities

Complete the answers to these questions:

1 Outline three ways in which Muslims prepare for *salah*.

To prepare for prayer, Muslims must find a clean place which faces Makkah, remove their shoes and ....

....

2 Explain two reasons why *jummah* prayers are important for Muslims. In your answer you must refer to a source of wisdom and authority.

Jummah prayers are important for Muslims because they provide an opportunity for the local Muslim community to meet together and receive advice and spiritual guidance from the imam.

Jummah prayers are also important because they have been commanded by God in the Qur'an, which means good Muslims will perform them. Surah 62 says that ....

Exam support

You might be asked to evaluate a statement such as:

Christian and Muslim worship is very similar.

The table below might help you answer such questions.

Arguments for	Arguments against
Worship involves the whole congregation saying set prayers together (especially in the Christian Eucharist, but even non-liturgical services include the Lord's Prayer).	Muslims must face Makkah in worship whereas Christians face the east or any direction.
Weekly worship in both faiths includes a sermon.	Muslim worship must be in Arabic, but Christian worship is in the native language.
Worship in both faiths involves praying for the needs of others.	Men and women are separated in Muslim worship but not in Christian worship.
Worship in both faiths involves praising the one God.	Muslims must perform *wudu* before worshipping, but Christians do not have special preparations.

Topic 2.3.4 *Sawm*

REVISED

Sawm is the fourth pillar and means fasting. Muslims can fast voluntarily at any time, but the month of Ramadan is the compulsory month of fasting. All Muslims above the age of puberty should fast, though there are special exemptions.

Sawm means no food, drink, smoking, lying, gossiping, swearing, getting angry or sex from dawn to dusk. Families have two special meals a day, the ***iftar*** to break the fast at night and the ***suhur*** just before dawn to give strength to face the day's fast. Extra prayers are said and one-thirtieth of the Qur'an is read each day so that at the end of Ramadan the whole Qur'an has been read.

Ramadan had been a traditional holy month in Arabia, but Muhammad made sure that Ramadan was no longer connected with Makkan polytheism by using the lunar calendar, so that over a period of 32 years it moves through all the seasons. (This causes major problems in the UK and further north, when Ramadan falls in May, June and July.)

Sawm is important for Muslims because:

- keeping the fast enables the fourth pillar of Islam to be fulfilled
- the Qur'an is the greatest gift God has for humanity and keeping the fast in Ramadan is a way of thanking God for the Qur'an
- fasting brings Muslims closer to God so they can concentrate on God rather than the ordinary things of life
- fasting promotes self-control which a Muslim needs to practise their faith properly
- fasting in Ramadan unites and strengthens the Muslim community
- Ramadan brings Muslim families together and strengthens their bonds.

Destiny – what has been set out to happen

Iftar – the meal breaking the fast at night

Laylat al-Qadr – the Night of Power (destiny)

Suhur – the meal just before fasting starts at dawn

Laylat al-Qadr

All Muslims try to attend mosque on the 27th of Ramadan as this is ***Laylat al-Qad'r*** (translated as either the 'Night of Power and Excellence' or the 'Night of **Destiny**') – to celebrate the night when Muhammad received the first revelation of the Qur'an. Muslims celebrate with special prayers and read the Qur'an.

The Night of Power and Excellence is important for Muslims today because:

- it commemorates and celebrates the revelation of the Qur'an, the final and unalterable word of God
- it commemorates and celebrates the calling of Muhammad to be the last and final messenger of God to the world
- some Muslims believe this was the day Muhammad made his night journey to heaven (*al Mi'raj*) when God gave him the details of *salah*
- some Muslims, especially Shi'as, believe it is the Night of Destiny, when God decides everything that will happen in the coming year
- praying on that night is the best prayer (a hadith says it is better than praying for a thousand months)
- praying in the mosque on *Laylat al-Qadr* can bring forgiveness of all a person's sins.

Sources of wisdom and authority

- Surah 2 says that Muslims must fast for a set number of days during Ramadan to learn self-restraint.
- Surah 96 (the first revelation) says: 'On the Night of Power, Muhammad was commanded by God, 'Proclaim in the name of thy Lord and Cherisher, who created, created man out of a clot of congealed blood'.

Now test yourself

TESTED

1 The meal breaking the fast at night is called:
  a) *suhur*
  b) *iftar*
  c) *Laylat al-Qadr*
  d) *sirah*
2 The Night of Power and Excellence is known as:
  a) *suhur*
  b) *iftar*
  c) *Laylat al-Qadr*
  d) *sirah*
3 The Arabic for fasting is:
  a) *suhur*
  b) *iftar*
  c) *Laylat al-Qadr*
  d) *sawm*
4 The meal just before fasting starts at dawn is called:
  a) *suhur*
  b) *iftar*
  c) *Laylat al-Qadr*
  d) *sirah*

Activities

Complete the answers to these questions:

1 Outline three things Muslims must not do in daylight hours during Ramadan.

During Ramadan, Muslims must not eat any food in daylight hours. Also they must not consume liquids. A third thing they must not do is ....

2 Explain two reasons why Muslims fast during Ramadan. In your answer you must refer to a source of wisdom and authority.

Muslims fast during Ramadan because the Qur'an is the greatest gift God has given humanity and keeping the fast in Ramadan is a way of thanking God for the Qur'an. Muslims also fast because doing so brings them closer to God, allowing them to concentrate on God rather than the ordinary things of life.

Keeping the fast is fulfilling the fourth pillar of Islam and is commanded by God. Surah 2 says that Muslims must ....

Exam support

You might be asked to evaluate a statement such as:

One night in Ramadan is no more important than another.

The table below might help you answer such a question.

Arguments for	Arguments against
Some Muslims (especially Shi'as) think *Laylat al-Qadr* is the most important day because it commemorates and celebrates the revelation of the Qur'an.	Ramadan is a whole month of fasting which is prescribed in the Qur'an.
Laylat al-Qadr commemorates and celebrates the calling of Muhammad to be the last and final messenger of God.	One-thirtieth of the Qur'an is read each day so that the whole Qur'an is read in the month, so each day is equally important.
Laylat al-Qadr is the Night of Destiny when God decides everything that will happen in the coming year.	Fasting for the whole month (not one day) is what brings forgiveness of sins.
Praying on the night of *Laylat al-Qadr* is the best prayer because a hadith says it is better than praying for a thousand months.	The Qur'an makes no mention of any special days during Ramadan.

Topic 2.3.5 *Zakah* and *khums*

REVISED

Zakah

Zakah is the third pillar of Islam and is an annual tax on wealth. The Qur'an does not specify exactly how much tax should be paid so Sunni Muslims follow the Shari'ah, which sets out a ***nisab*** (the minimum people need to have before they have to pay *zakah*). A Muslim subtracts their outgoings from their assets and income and if what is left over is more than the *nisab*, then they pay 2.5 per cent of that amount as *zakah*. Many Muslims pay their *zakah* direct to Muslim charities such as Islamic Relief and Muslim Aid. Every mosque also has a *zakah* committee that collects the tax and distributes it according to the wishes of the mosque committee.

Special *zakahs* are paid on Id-ul-Fitr and on Id-ul-Adha, when a donation is often given to charity rather than sharing meat with the poor.

Zakah is used for orphans, widows, the poor, the homeless, tax collectors and religious purposes, such as Muslim schools and new mosques.

Muslims pay *zakah* because:

- it is the third pillar of Islam, which all Muslims must fulfil
- paying *zakah* is a sign of a Muslim's submission to God
- *zakah* means purification. Islam teaches that wealth can be evil and cut people off from God, but if a Muslim pays *zakah* they purify the wealth they have left
- some scholars teach that God is more likely to accept prayers if the person praying pays *zakah*.

Alms – charitable giving to the poor

Khums – paid by the Shi'a, it is a tax of 20 per cent on profits

Nisab – the amount of income or wealth a Muslim needs to have before they are liable to *zakah*

Sadaqah – voluntary giving to the poor

Sadaqah

Islam also puts forward the idea of voluntary giving to charity. This is known as ***sadaqah*** because it is voluntary, whereas *zakah* is compulsory. *Zakah* aims to reduce the gap between the rich and the poor and so Muslims should give voluntary *sadaqah* in addition to *zakah* to help the poor.

Khums

The Shari'ah for Shi'a Muslims only refers to paying *zakah* on agricultural products, gold and silver, which no longer apply to most people, and so for the Shi'a, the tax of ***khums*** (one fifth of a gain) has become more important.

Khums is based on Surah 8:41: 'Know that whatever of a thing you acquire, a fifth of it is for Allah …'. *Khums* is applied to business profit or surplus, and 20 per cent of surplus income must be paid as *khums*. Fifty per cent of *khums* money goes to religious causes and fifty per cent goes in the form of **alms** to the poor, orphans and the homeless. This means that 10 per cent of business income goes to religious leaders and descendants of the Prophet. Shi'as pay *khums* because it is commanded in the Qur'an and this money provides a major source of income for religious leaders in the Shi'a community.

Sunnis do not pay *khums* because they think 'whatever of a thing you acquire' refers only to the spoils of war.

Sources of wisdom and authority

- With regard to the amount of *zakah*, Surah 2 says, 'Whatever ye spend, that is good'.
- Surah 9:60 says that *zakah* should be spent on the poor and the needy, recent converts, in the cause of God and for travellers.
- Muhammad said in a hadith that giving *zakah* protects a Muslim's property and helps relatives to recover from disease.

Now test yourself

TESTED

1 Charitable giving to the poor is known as:
   a) *nisab*
   b) alms
   c) *khums*
   d) *sadaqah*
2 The Shi'a tax of 20 per cent on profits is:
   a) *nisab*
   b) alms
   c) *khums*
   d) *sadaqah*
3 The amount of income or wealth a Muslim needs to have before they are liable to *zakah* is:
   a) *nisab*
   b) alms
   c) *khums*
   d) *sadaqah*
4 Voluntary giving to the poor is known by Muslims as:
   a) *nisab*
   b) alms
   c) *khums*
   d) *sadaqah*

Activities

Complete the answers to these questions:

1 Outline three groups that are helped by the *khums* charity tax.

Shi'a Muslims pay the khums tax to make sure that the descendants of Muhammad are properly cared for. Another group the tax helps is religious leaders. A third group is ....

2 Explain two reasons why Muslims pay *zakah*. In your answer you must refer to a source of wisdom and authority.

Muslims pay zakah to purify their wealth (zakah means purification). Islam teaches that wealth can be evil and cut people off from God, but if a Muslim pays zakah, they purify the wealth they have left and God will accept their prayers.

Muslims also pay zakah because it is the third pillar of Islam which all Muslims must fulfil. Muhammad said in a hadith that zakah ....

Exam support

You might be asked to evaluate a statement such as:

Zakah *and* khums *alone will never solve the problems of poverty.*

The table below might help you answer such a question.

Arguments for	Arguments against
Zakah is only 2.5 per cent of taxable income, whereas people in the UK pay about 30 per cent of their income in tax and there is still poverty.	Many Muslims pay their *zakah* directlly to Muslim charities such as Islamic Relief and Muslim Aid.
Khums only applies to business profits and in the UK businesses pay more than 20 per cent tax on their profits.	Special *zakahs* are paid on Id-ul-Fitr and on Id-ul-Adha when a donation is often given to charity rather than sharing meat with the poor.
The special *zakahs* bring in a very small amount compared with the tax receipts in a country like the UK.	*Zakah* is used for orphans, widows, the poor and the homeless.
There is more poverty in countries operating strict Shari'ah than in countries operating European taxation laws.	*Khums* is 20 per cent of business profit or surplus, and 50 per cent of *khums* goes to the poor, orphans and the homeless.

Topic 2.3.6 *Hajj*

REVISED

Hajj is the fifth pillar and takes place in **Dhu al-Hijah**. Muslims can only go on *hajj* if they can provide for their dependants while they are on *hajj*, and they are physically and mentally fit. While on *hajj* Muslims must wear ***ihram***, the pilgrim dress.

Most events take place in the Great Mosque of Makkah, which contains the **Ka'aba**.

The events of *hajj*

- Day 1 – pilgrims **circumambulate** the Ka'aba seven times while saying the ***talbiya*** prayer (this is called a ***tawaf***). Then they do seven circuits of the **Ma'sa** (the covered passageway between two hills, which pilgrims run between) and return to the main courtyard for midday prayer.
- Day 2 – pilgrims are given water from the **Zamzam well** and then walk 11 miles to **Arafat**.
- Day 3 – the ***Waquf*** of Arafat – pilgrims stand on the plain in front of the hill of Arafat and confess their sins. Any pilgrims who miss the *Waquf* of Arafat must repeat *hajj*.
- Day 4 – pilgrims throw stones at the stoning pillars (these represent Satan and remind the pilgrims that Satan tempted Ibrahim to disobey God). Then the pilgrims offer a sacrifice to God, remembering how God provided a sacrifice for Ibrahim after he obeyed God by being prepared to sacrifice his son. Groups of pilgrims get together to buy an animal for sacrifice – they are then expected to eat some and send the rest to the poor. This is the part of *hajj* that all Muslims throughout the world join in as the festival of Id-ul-Adha.
- Days 5–7 – pilgrims stone the pillars.
- Day 8 – pilgrims walk to Makkah and perform a final *tawaf* and circuit of the Ma'sa. The pilgrims have then completed *hajj*.

Anyone who completes *hajj* is known as a ***hajji*** and they may colour their hair or beard with henna as a sign of their status. Hajjis receive particular respect from the Muslim community.

The main reasons for going on *hajj* are:

- to fulfil the final pillar and so complete a Muslim life
- to follow the example of Muhammad by performing the actions he performed in the places he performed them
- to visit the holiest sites of Islam and feel part of their holiness.

The significance of *hajj*

Hajj has great significance for Muslims because a pilgrim:

- has fulfilled the fifth pillar as set down in Surah 22 and so can die happy
- has followed the example and actions of the Prophet in the very places the Prophet himself performed them
- has taken part in the holiest event in Islam and has come as close to God as is possible in this life
- is made aware of the power of God to unite different races and languages into a common language, a common ritual and a common brotherhood in Islam
- has their sins forgiven so they now live life as a perfect Muslim.

Arafat – the plain and hill 11 miles from Makkah where the central part of *hajj* takes place

Circumambulate – walk round, make a circuit

Dhu al-Hijja – the twelfth month of the Islamic calendar, when *hajj* takes place

Hajji – one who has completed the *hajj*

Ihram – pilgrim dress

Ka'aba – (or Ka'ba) the House of God in Makkah containing the black stone

Ma'sa – the covered passageway between the hills Marwa and Safa, which pilgrims run between

Tawaf – seven circuits of the Ka'aba

Waquf – a standing prayer during *hajj*

Zamzam well – the well in the courtyard of the Great Mosque given by God for Hagar and Ismail

Sources of wisdom and authority

- Surah 22 says that Muslims should go on pilgrimage, complete the rites prescribed for them, perform their vows, and circumambulate the Ka'aba.
- In his final sermon given on his final *hajj*, Muhammad said, 'All the believers are brothers ... none is higher than the other unless he is higher in obedience to Allah'.

Now test yourself

TESTED

1 The standing prayer during *hajj* is called:
   a) Dhu al-Hijja
   b) *ihram*
   c) *tawaf*
   d) *Waquf*

2 Seven circuits of the Ka'aba are:
   a) Dhu al-Hijja
   b) *ihram*
   c) *tawaf*
   d) *Waquf*

3 The twelfth month of the Islamic calendar when *hajj* takes place is:
   a) Dhu al-Hijja
   b) *ihram*
   c) *tawaf*
   d) *Waquf*

4 Pilgrim dress is called:
   a) Dhu al-Hijja
   b) *ihram*
   c) *tawaf*
   d) *Waquf*

Activities

Complete the answers to these questions:

1 Outline three features of *hajj* which show the unity of Islam.

While they are on hajj, all pilgrims must wear the same pilgrim dress. They must all use the same language and ....

2 Explain two reasons why *hajj* is important for Muslims. In your answer you must refer to a source of wisdom and authority.

Hajj is important for Muslims because it is the holiest event in Islam when Muslims come as close to God as is possible in this life. The sacred presence they experience momentarily during salah prayers is believed to be present for the whole duration of hajj.

Another reason why hajj is important is that once they have been on hajj, Muslims have completed all five of the pillars and so can die happy. Surah 22 says that Muslims should ....

....

Exam support

You might be asked to evaluate a statement such as:

Hajj *has more benefits than drawbacks.*

The table below might help you answer such a question.

Arguments for	Arguments against
Hajj allows a Muslim to follow the example of Muhammad, performing the actions he performed in the places he performed them.	*Hajj* attracts huge crowds and this can lead to accidents and even death – over 1,800 people were crushed to death in the stampede at the 2015 *hajj*.
On *hajj* a Muslim visits the holiest sites of Islam and can feel part of their holiness.	Language can cause a problem, for example many of the people killed in 2015 would not have been able to understand the Arabic of the Saudi controllers.
Anyone who completes *hajj* is known as a *hajji* and will receive special respect from the Muslim community.	During *hajj*, the rich and powerful receive preferential treatment, which many feel is hypocritical since everyone is supposed to be equal.
Hajj is the final pillar and so completes a Muslim life.	Going on *hajj* costs a lot of money, so it is unfair that such a holy event is unlikely to be available to the poor.

Topic 2.3.7 *Jihad*

REVISED

The word *jihad* means 'to strive, to apply oneself, to struggle, to persevere', but Muslims believe it means 'struggling in the way of religion' or 'striving in the cause of God'. Determining exactly what is meant by the cause of God has led to two ideas about *jihad*: greater *jihad* and lesser *jihad*.

Greater *jihad*

Most Muslims believe that the greater *jihad* is the struggle to make oneself a perfect Muslim. The struggle is:

- to perform all of the Five Pillars properly
- to follow the Shari'ah exactly
- to both discover and follow the perfect example of the Prophet Muhammad
- to be 'pleasing to Allah', so that one will be allowed into paradise.

Most Muslim lawyers teach that the greater *jihad* is striving to uphold all of God's commandments and striving to condemn all of God's prohibitions before one can embark on removing evil from the world.

Lesser *jihad*

Having removed the evil from themselves, Muslims can then begin to remove the evil from society. Muslim lawyers teach that this should start with Muslim societies by tackling underdevelopment, the lack of education and the gap between rich and poor to produce perfect Muslim societies. Only then can they target non-Muslim societies and bring them into Islam.

According to Islam, it is God's law and Islamic teaching that will bring about world peace.

Lesser Jihad is not a Holy War against non-Muslims. An Islamic Holy War can only be fought:

- in self-defence
- if it is led by a religious leader well known for piety and chosen by the whole community
- if all the soldiers are good faithful Muslims, well versed in the Qur'an
- if there is a good chance of the war being successful
- as long as the war does not harm the innocent (women, children or the elderly).

Halal – that which is permitted

Haram – that which is not permitted

Muslim Law Schools – the four schools which interpret the Shari'ah for Sunni Muslims

Ummah – the Muslim community (brotherhood of Islam)

The importance of *jihad* in the life of Muslims

Being a good Muslim involves a lot of struggle, so the idea of *jihad* is very important to Muslims. Muslims living in a non-Muslim country must avoid being involved in the payment of interest and must ensure that they keep to the ***halal*** (permitted) and avoid the ***haram*** (banned). This can be a particular struggle in regard to finding *halal* food, and avoiding alcohol and gambling in their daily life.

Keeping the Five Pillars is also difficult, especially when living in a non-Muslim country.

So *jihad* is important because everyday life makes it a *jihad* to be a good Muslim.

Sources of wisdom and authority

- Surah 22 says that those who strive in God's cause will be guided by God because God is with those who do right.
- Surah 2 says that Muslims must fight in self-defence, but must keep to God's rules.

Now test yourself

TESTED

1 That which is permitted is:
- a) *ummah*
- b) *halal*
- c) *haram*
- d) *jihad*

2 That which is not permitted is:
- a) *ummah*
- b) *halal*
- c) *haram*
- d) *jihad*

3 Striving in the cause of God is:
- a) *ummah*
- b) *halal*
- c) *haram*
- d) *jihad*

4 The Muslim community is called the:
- a) *ummah*
- b) *halal*
- c) *haram*
- d) *jihad*

Activities

Complete the answers to these questions:

1 Outline three ways in which being a Muslim in a non-Muslim society is a struggle.

A Muslim living in a non-Muslim country faces a considerable struggle to avoid being involved in the payment of interest. It can also be a great struggle to find halal food, especially halal meat.

Another struggle is ....

2 Explain two reasons why there are different understandings of *jihad* in Islam. In your answer you must refer to a source of wisdom and authority.

The Muslim belief in jihad is based on surahs of the Qur'an such as Surah 22, which says that those who strive in God's cause will be guided by God because God is with those who do right.

Jihad is 'striving in the cause of God', but Muslims understand this differently. Some Muslims think it means striving to make yourself a good Muslim, while others think ....

....

....

....

....

....

....

Exam support

You might be asked to evaluate a statement such as:

Jihad *is about making yourself a good Muslim, not fighting wars.*

The table below might help you answer such a question.

Arguments for	Arguments against
Jihad means struggle and it is a struggle to make oneself a perfect Muslim.	Some Muslims believe strive means fight and they believe *jihad* is about fighting wars because the Qur'an says that Muslims must fight if they are attacked.
Most Muslim lawyers teach that the greater *jihad* is striving to uphold all of God's commandments and to condemn all God's prohibitions before embarking on removing evil from the world.	Some Muslims believe strive means fight because Muhammad fought in wars.
If you are not a good Muslim and you attack others for not being good Muslims, you are a hypocrite, which is condemned in the Qur'an.	There are many hadith from Muhammad which say that Muslims should fight in Just Wars.
Islam means peace and so it cannot be about fighting wars.	The Qur'an says that Muslims dying in a Just War will go straight to heaven.

Topic 2.3.8 Celebrations and commemorations

REVISED

The festival of Id-ul-Adha

On Id-ul-Adha, there is a special *khutba* (sermon) in the mosque when the people are reminded of the origins of the festival and united with the pilgrims in Makkah performing *hajj*. A special *zakah* is given to the poor as part of the sacrifice of *hajj*.

This festival originates from the occasion when God tested Ibrahim by asking him to sacrifice his son Ismail, but when God saw Ibrahim obeying him, God sent an animal sacrifice instead. During Id-ul-Adha, Muslims feel they are sharing in the *hajj*, symbolically sacrificing themselves to God and sharing the good things of life with the poor.

Amir al-Mu'minin – commander of the faithful, a title given by Shi'as to Ali and his descendants

Ghadeer of Khum – the Pool of Khum halfway between Makkah and Madinah

Husayn – Muhammad's grandson and the third Imam of Shi'a Islam

Karbala – site of the battle where Husayn was killed by Caliph Yazid (60 miles south-west of Baghdad)

The festival of Id-ul-Fitr

Id-ul-Fitr signals the end of the fast of Ramadan. Cards and gifts are exchanged, and new clothes are bought for children. Special services are held in the mosque, thanking God for the benefits of Ramadan, with a *khutba* reminding Muslims of the meaning of Ramadan. A special meal is shared – the first daylight meal for a month.

Muslims celebrate Id-ul-Fitr because it means:

- Ramadan has ended and they have completed a great religious feat and will gain many benefits
- their sins have been forgiven
- they have become close to God.

The commemoration of Id-ul-Ghadeer

This festival celebrates Muhammad appointing Ali as his successor. Shi'as celebrate by fasting, ritual bathing and having a special service when a sermon is preached on the event and special prayers are said, after which food is given to poor Muslims.

Shi'as claim that on his way back to Madinah from his final pilgrimage, Muhammad met Ali at the **Ghadeer of Khum** (Pool of Khum), and appointed Ali as his successor. Shi'a Muslims call Ali **Amir al-Mu'minin**, commander of the faithful.

This event is very important to Shi'a Muslims because it means that Ali should have been the first Caliph and Shi'as are the true followers of Muhammad because they have followed his request to regard Ali as Muhammad's true successor.

Sunni Muslims reject this view and do not celebrate the festival.

The commemoration of Ashura

Ashura is a remembrance, not a celebration. It remembers Muhammad's grandson, **Husayn**, being killed (murdered by Caliph Yazid) at the Battle of **Karbala**. Shi'a Muslims wear mourning clothes, refrain from music, fast and mourn for Husayn. They participate in public processions when they whip themselves as a sign of their devotion.

Ashura is important to Shi'as because the mourning washes away sins and allows them to show their devotion to the Imams and the forces of good, and remember the betrayal of Islam by the Sunnis.

Sources of wisdom and authority

- At the sermon given on Id-ul-Fitr, Muslims are told that: 'The religious duties of the first ten days of Ramadan gain the mercy of God, those of the second ten merit his pardon, while those of the last ten save those who do them from the punishment of hell.'
- A hadith says that Muhammad said that Muslims should eat some of the sacrifice of Id-ul-Adha and use the rest to help the needy.
- A Shi'a hadith about Ashura says: 'A single tear shed for Husayn washes away a hundred sins.'

Now test yourself

TESTED ☐

1 Husayn is:
   a) the commander of the faithful, a title given by Shi'as to Ali and his descendants
   b) the Pool of Khum, halfway between Makkah and Madinah
   c) Muhammad's grandson and the third Imam of Shi'a Islam
   d) the site of the battle where Husayn was killed
2 Karbala is:
   a) the commander of the faithful, a title given by Shi'as to Ali and his descendants
   b) the Pool of Khum, halfway between Makkah and Madinah
   c) Muhammad's grandson and the third Imam of Shi'a Islam
   d) the site of the battle where Husayn was killed
3 Amir al-Mu'minin is:
   a) the commander of the faithful, a title given by Shi'as to Ali and his descendants
   b) the Pool of Khum, halfway between Makkah and Madinah
   c) Muhammad's grandson and the third Imam of Shi'a Islam
   d) the site of the battle where Husayn was killed
4 Ghadeer Khum is:
   a) the commander of the faithful, a title given by Shi'as to Ali and his descendants
   b) the Pool of Khum, halfway between Makkah and Madinah
   c) Muhammad's grandson and the third Imam of Shi'a Islam
   d) the site of the battle where Husayn was killed

Activities

Complete the answers to these questions:

1 Outline three things Muslim do to celebrate Id-ul-Fitr.

Cards and gifts are exchanged, and new clothes are bought for children. Special services are held in the mosque with special prayers thanking God for the benefits of Ramadan. A third thing Muslims do is ....

....

2 Explain two reasons why Muslims celebrate Id-ul-Adha. In your answer you must refer to a source of wisdom and authority.

Muslims celebrate Id-ul-Adha because it is a chance for them to join in the hajj as the pilgrims remember when God tested Ibrahim by asking him to sacrifice his son Ismail, but when God saw Ibrahim obeying him, God sent an animal sacrifice instead.

Another reason is that during Id-ul-Adha Muslims feel they are symbolically sacrificing themselves to God, sharing the good things of life with the poor. Muhammad said that Muslims should eat some of the sacrifice and ....

Exam support

You might be asked to evaluate a statement such as: *Religious celebrations cause nothing but trouble.*

The table below might help you answer such a question.

Arguments for	Arguments against
In 2009, dozens of people were killed and hundreds injured in a bomb explosion at the Ashura procession in Karachi, Pakistan.	Id-ul-Adha brings Muslims together as they celebrate the unity of the Islamic *ummah*.
In 2011, a hundred Shi'as were killed by a series of bomb attacks on the day of Ashura observation.	Id-ul-Fitr brings Shi'a and Sunni Muslims together as they celebrate the ending of Ramadan together.
In 2006, Christians were attacked during a Hindu festival in Gujarat state.	Christmas brings peace to different Christian groups and different nationalities.
Historically the Easter story has been used to justify anti Jewish feelings.	The pilgrimage to Makkah brings Sunnis and Shi'as together as a united faith, wearing the same clothes, performing the same actions and speaking the same language.

2.4 Peace and conflict

Topic 2.4.1 Muslim attitudes towards peace

REVISED

Islam, a religion of peace

The word 'Islam' is derived from '*aslama*', which means to surrender or submit, so Islam is the religion of submission to the will of God. However, the consonants '*s-l-m*' are those of '***salaam***', which means peace, so there is a close connection between Islam and peace. Indeed, one meaning of the word 'Islam' is peace. The greeting used by all Muslims when they meet each other is '***salaam alaykum***' – 'May peace be with you.'

Followers of Islam believe that their religion brings them a peaceful life, which comes about when they obey God's call and live by the moral values set by God, so that compassion, mercy, peace and love can be experienced all over the world. Muslims refer to those countries where Islam is the national religion as 'the abode of peace', while countries outside Islam are called 'the abode of war'.

One of the attributes of God described in the Qur'an is 'peace and security', which means that for Muslims, God's being itself is a manifestation of peace. According to Surah 5:16, **divine guidance** is like a path of peace and paradise. Paradise, an abode of peace, is the ultimate destination for Muslims: 'For them will be a home of peace in the presence of their Lord' (Surah 6:127).

Peace is important for Muslims because:

- Islam teaches that accepting Islam brings inner peace through submitting to the will of Allah
- when Muslims have inner peace it encourages them to have peaceful relationships with other people
- the Qur'an calls Islam '**Dar as Salaam**' – the House of Peace
- Islam teaches that true peace both within and between people comes from accepting Islam and living its ways
- the Qur'an tells Muslims that, 'an **amicable** settlement … is best'
- the hadith say that whenever the Prophet had an option between two courses of action, he always chose the non-confrontational one.

Amicable – peaceful and friendly

Dar as Salaam – the House of Peace

Divine guidance – being shown what to do by God

Salaam – peace

Salaam alaykum – the Muslim equivalent of hello which means peace be with you

Sources of wisdom and authority

- The Qur'an says that God guides good people 'to ways of peace and safety'.
- There is a hadith which says that Muhammad said, 'War is a deception'.

Now test yourself

TESTED

1 A word meaning peaceful or friendly:
   a) *Salaam alaykum*
   b) *Salaam*
   c) Dar as Salaam
   d) Amicable
2 A phrase meaning the House of Peace:
   a) *Salaam alaykum*
   b) *Salaam*
   c) Dar as Salaam
   d) Amicable
3 A word meaning peace:
   a) *Salaam alaykum*
   b) *Salaam*
   c) Dar as Salaam
   d) Amicable
4 The Muslim equivalent of hello:
   a) *Salaam alaykum*
   b) *Salaam*
   c) Dar as Salaam
   d) Amicable

Activities

Complete the answers to these questions:

1 Outline three facts which show Islam is a religion of peace.

One fact is that the word 'Islam' comes from the consonants s-l-m which form the Arabic word for peace, salaam. Another fact is that Muslims say 'peace be with you' instead of 'hello'. A third fact is that Islam is known as 'Dar as Salaam', which means ....

2 Explain two reasons why Muslims believe that Islam is a religion of peace. In your answer you must refer to a source of wisdom and authority.

Muslims believe Islam is a religion of peace since the word 'Islam' is derived from the word which means 'peace' in Arabic. Muslims describe countries where Islam is the national religion as 'the abode of peace' and countries outside Islam are called 'the abode of war'.

One of the attributes of God described in the Qur'an is 'peace and security', which means that for Muslims, God's being itself is a manifestation of peace. The Qur'an says that divine guidance is like a path of peace and paradise, while the ultimate destination for Muslims is an abode of peace. As Surah 6 says, ...

Exam support

You might be asked to evaluate a statement such as: *Islam is the House of Peace.*

The table below might help you answer such a question.

Arguments for	Arguments against
Islam teaches that accepting Islam brings inner peace through submitting to the will of Allah.	The Qur'an says that Muslims must fight if they are attacked.
When Muslims have inner peace it encourages them to have peaceful relationships with other people.	Muhammad fought in wars.
The Qur'an calls Islam 'Dar as Salaam' – the House of Peace – and says that 'God doth call to the Home of Peace: He doth guide whom He pleaseth to a way that is straight'.	There are many hadith from Muhammad saying Muslims should fight in Just Wars.
Islam teaches that true peace 'both within and between people' comes from accepting Islam and living according to its ways.	There are plenty of areas around the world where extremist Muslims are claiming that their faith justifies their attacks on non-believers.

Topic 2.4.2 The role of Muslims in peacemaking

REVISED

Islam recommends its followers to be peacemakers, because this is the teaching of the Qur'an. According to the Qur'an, Muslims should seek to end disagreements by making peace rather than starting further disputes and fights.

Muslims believe that justice is an important part of peacemaking because if a society and its laws are unjust:

- People will campaign against them, which will lead to trouble in society (e.g. the civil rights campaign in the southern United States in the 1960s disrupted normal life).
- People may start a civil war (e.g. in Syria where the Sunni Muslims began a civil war because they thought the **Alawi** Assad regime laws were treating them unfairly).

Muslims believe forgiveness and reconciliation are important in peacemaking because:

- God is compassionate and merciful to sinners, and so Muslims should be merciful and forgiving to those who cause them offence.
- Muslims cannot ask for God's forgiveness on the Day of Judgement if they are not prepared to forgive.
- The Qur'an says that Muslims should forgive other people's sins against them.
- There are many hadith from the Prophet Muhammad about forgiving people who have offended others and bringing **reconciliation** to conflicts.

Ahmadiyya – a Muslim sect founded in Pakistan that is against war

Alawi – a Twelver Shi'a group which is part of the ruling group in Syria

Justice – the allocation of due reward and punishment

Prophetic *jihad* – *jihad* as understood and practised by the Prophet Muhammad

Reconciliation – bringing together people who were opposed to each other

Muslims working for peace today

The **Ahmadiyya** Movement began in Pakistan but has relocated its headquarters to London because of persecution in Pakistan. The Ahmadiyya work for peace by:

- having the motto 'Love for all, hatred for none' on all their publications
- holding an annual peace symposium about how Islam could come together with other religions and tackle the causes of war and terrorism
- campaigning for human rights for everyone, whatever their religion, especially in Muslim countries
- speaking out against any terrorist activities perpetrated in the name of Islam.

The Muslim Peace Fellowship (MPF) is another organisation dedicated to Islamic non-violence and believes that **prophetic *jihad*** is the struggle to make a wise, just and compassionate society. The objectives of the MPF are as follows:

- To work against injustice and for peace in ourselves, our families, our communities, and our world.
- To affirm the commitment to peace on behalf of all Muslims.
- To explore and deepen our understanding of Islamic teachings about peace and nonviolence.
- To reach out to people of other religious traditions to further mutual understanding and respect, and to build solidarity in the service of the planet.

Sources of wisdom and authority

- The Qur'an says that Muslims are a single brotherhood who should make peace and reconciliation whenever there are quarrels.
- 'Let there be no compulsion in religion.' (Surah 2)

Now test yourself

TESTED

1 A Muslim sect opposed to war is:
 a) *al'Jannah*
 b) Ahmadiyya
 c) Alawi
 d) Al-Hijra

2 A Twelver Shi'a group (part of the ruling group in Syria) is:
 a) *al'Jannah*
 b) Ahmadiyya
 c) Alawi
 d) Al-Hijra

3 The allocation of due reward and punishment is:
 a) justice
 b) judicial
 c) redemption
 d) reconciliation

4 Bringing together people who were opposed to each other is:
 a) justice
 b) judicial
 c) redemption
 d) reconciliation

Activities

Complete the answers to these questions:

1 Outline three ways in which a Muslim group works for peace.

The Ahmadiyya Muslims work for peace by holding an annual peace symposium about how Islam could come together with other religions and tackle the causes of war and terrorism. They campaign for human rights for everyone, whatever their religion, especially in Muslim countries. They also ....

2 Explain two reasons why forgiveness and reconciliation are important for Muslims. In your answer you must refer to a source of wisdom and authority.

Forgiveness and reconciliation are important for Muslims because the Qur'an teaches that God is compassionate and merciful to sinners, and so Muslims should be merciful and forgiving to those who cause them offence.

There are many hadith from the Prophet Muhammad about bringing reconciliation to conflicts. The Qur'an says that ....
....

Exam support

You might be asked to evaluate a statement such as: *There can be no peace without justice.*

The table below might help you answer such a question.

Arguments for	Arguments against
People cannot live at peace if society and its laws are unjust – an example is the civil rights campaign in the southern United States in the 1960s.	Muslims can live at peace regardless of whether they have justice because Muslims believe Islam brings a peaceful life.
The civil war in Syria (2011–present) began because the Sunni Muslims were being treated unjustly by the Alawi Assad regime.	One of the attributes of God described in the Qur'an is 'peace and security', which means that, for Muslims, God's being itself is a manifestation of peace.
The war and terrorism in Palestine has been ongoing for 70 years because the Palestinians feel they are being treated unjustly by Israel.	Islam teaches that accepting Islam brings inner peace through submitting to the will of Allah.
The war and terrorism in Kashmir has been ongoing for 70 years because the Muslims feel they are being treated unjustly by India.	When Muslims have inner peace it encourages them to have peaceful relationships with other people.

Topic 2.4.3 Attitudes to conflict

REVISED

War and conflict causes many problems:

- Death and injury – this is the most obvious problem of war and conflict, especially for civilian populations. For example, to date there have been 400,000 deaths in the Syrian civil war.
- Refugees – the UNHCR (the office of the United Nations High Commissioner for Refugees) is currently looking after more than 16 million refugees.
- Economic problems – wars disrupt the economy of the countries involved in the conflict and cause social and economic problems in the countries where the refugees end up.

Some of the most common reasons for wars to occur are:

- Religion – differences in religion often lead to war.
- Nationalism/**ethnicity** – one form of nationalism is when different ethnic groups think they should have their own country because they have a different culture. Another type of nationalism is the idea that minority ethnic groups should be removed from a country so that the nation is made up of only one ethnic group.
- Resources – conflict can occur when one country has resources that another country wants or needs, such as oil or water.

Muslim responses to the causes of war

Most Muslims believe that if a war is just then a Muslim must fight in it. Muhammad, the perfect exemplar for Muslims, fought in wars of self-defence.

However, Muslims must be very clear about the causes of the conflict. Muslims should not fight in wars:

- where they could be classed as the aggressor
- where resources are being taken from someone else
- that are forcing another country or people to become Muslim.

Muslims should always be wary of going to war because Muhammad himself said that 'war is a deception', meaning it is never what it seems. However, the Qur'an says Muslims must fight if they are attacked.

Ethnicity – having the characteristics of a certain race or culture

Ethnic cleansing – the mass expulsion or killing of members of one ethnic or religious group in an area by those of another

Atheist and Humanist responses to the causes of war

Most Humanists believe that a good way to end wars is to get rid of religion. They believe that challenging religious leaders and believers can help to bring peace. Many Humanists are pacifists and so they would not fight in wars. Although many atheists have similar views about war as Humanists, some would be willing to fight in 'just' wars.

Situation Ethics and war

Muslims, Jews and Humanists often apply the idea of Situation Ethics to the issue of war. They will look at the causes and effects of a war and make a decision based upon what will produce the most loving outcome. For example, they may be against war but if a country has been invaded and its people are being wiped out (**ethnic cleansing**) they may decide the best solution is to declare war on the invaders. Similarly, people who think war can be justified may choose not to fight if they believe the end result will be nuclear weapons destroying the world.

Sources of wisdom and authority

- The Qur'an says that Muslims must fight in self-defence, but should keep to God's rules for fighting wars.
- There is a hadith which says that Muhammad said, 'War is a deception'.

Now test yourself

TESTED

1 Ethnicity means:
 a) belonging to a non-Christian religion
 b) belonging to a non-European racial group
 c) having the characteristics of a certain race or culture
 d) belonging to a certain group

2 Ethnic cleansing is:
 a) giving equal rights to all ethnic groups
 b) expelling from a country, or killing, the members of one ethnic or religious group
 c) giving superior rights to one ethnic or religious group
 d) discriminating against one ethnic or religious group

3 Internal displacement is:
 a) fleeing from war
 b) having to move your home within your country because of conflict
 c) becoming a refugee
 d) having to move to another country because of conflict

4 The UNHCR is:
 a) the office of the United Nations High Committee for Refugees
 b) the office of the United Nations High Condominium for Refugees
 c) the office of the United Nations High Commissioner for Refugees
 d) the office of the United Nations High Council for Refugees

Activities

Complete the answers to these questions:

1 Outline three problems caused by war.

A major problem of war is death and injury, especially among the civilian population. Another problem is that war leads to the displacement of people who then become refugees – the UNHCR is currently looking after more than 16 million war refugees. A third problem is ....

2 Explain two Muslim responses to war. In your answer you must refer to a source of wisdom and authority.

Most Muslims believe that if a war is just then a Muslim must fight in it. The Qur'an says Muslims must fight if they are attacked and Muhammad, the perfect exemplar for Muslims, fought in wars of self-defence. The Qur'an says that Muslims must fight in self-defence, but should keep to God's rules for fighting wars. However, some Muslims are not happy about fighting in wars because there is a hadith which says that
....

Exam support

You might be asked to evaluate a statement such as: *Religion is the main cause of wars.*

The table below might help you answer such a question.

Arguments for	Arguments against
The Qur'an says Muslims must fight if they are attacked: 'Fight in the cause of God those who fight you.' (Surah 2)	Ethnicity causes wars when different ethnic groups think they should have their own country, for example the ethnic Albanians in Kosovo.
Muhammad, the perfect exemplar for Muslims, fought in wars of self-defence.	Wars often occur if a country has resources that another country wants or needs, for example one reason why the two Gulf Wars occurred was so the West could retain its access to oil.
The Syrian civil war is a conflict between two different branches of Islam – Shi'as and Sunnis.	Religion is about peace not war: 'But if the enemy inclines towards peace, do thou also incline towards peace and trust in God'.
Several conflicts in Africa are between Christians and Muslims, for example in South Sudan and the Central African Republic.	Many religious groups are working for peace, for example the Ahmadiyya Muslims and the Muslim Peace Fellowship.

Topic 2.4.4 Pacifism

REVISED

Pacifism is opposition to war, **militarism** and violence.

Pacifism began in the Roman Empire when several Roman writers wrote books against war, but most modern pacifists base their ideas on the teachings of Jesus in his **Sermon on the Mount**. For the first 300 years of Christianity, Christians refused to fight in wars.

During the late nineteenth century, peace groups were formed and international peace congresses were held to promote pacifism and the end of war. Many pacifists became **conscientious objectors** during the two World Wars, and after the development of nuclear weapons they formed groups such as **CND** (Campaign for Nuclear Disarmament) in the UK and Peace Action in the USA to try to prevent a nuclear war.

Muslims and pacifism

Most Muslims would not agree with **passive resistance** because:

- the Qur'an encourages all Muslims to 'struggle in the way of Islam' and the Arabic word for struggle is *jihad*, which is often translated as 'fight'
- there is no idea of pacifism or turning the other cheek in Islam
- the Qur'an says that if Muslims are attacked, they must fight back.

However, there is a tradition of passive resistance in Islam:

- Surah 5:28 records that Moses and Aaron refused to fight the Israelites who had rebelled against God and instead separated themselves from them.
- Surah 23 says that Muslims should fight evil with good.
- The democratic movements in Middle Eastern countries in the Arab Spring of 2011 were based on pacifism and passive resistance, for example the demonstrations of passive resistance in Cairo succeeded in overthrowing President Mubarak and the rebellion in Tunisia was mainly non-violent.
- The Ahmadiyya are an example of a Muslim pacifist group.

Khan Abdul Ghaffar Khan (1890–1988) was a famous Muslim pacifist and a friend of Gandhi, who organised a non-violent movement to campaign for Indian independence from British rule. He was nominated for the Nobel Peace prize for his work for Muslim pacifism. He said to his followers, 'I am going to give you such a weapon that the police and the army will not be able to stand against it. It is the weapon of the Prophet, but you are not aware of it. That weapon is patience and righteousness. No power on earth can stand against it.'

Non-religious attitudes to pacifism

Humanists are opposed to war; many are pacifists and have been conscientious objectors during times of war. Humanists also helped to set up the United Nations. Those Humanists who are not pacifists would still give very careful consideration before supporting war because wars are hugely destructive, ruining lives, wasting resources and degrading the environment. Humanists believe that it is absurd to go to war and kill people in the name of religion. They also criticise the part that organised religions can sometimes play in encouraging and supporting wars.

CND – an organisation that promotes nuclear disarmament in the UK

Conscientious objector – a person who for reasons of conscience objects to serving in the armed forces

Militarism – belief that a country should have strong armed forces and be prepared to use them aggressively

Pacifism – opposition to war

Passive resistance – non-violent opposition to authority

Sermon on the Mount – Jesus' description of Christian living

Sources of wisdom and authority

- The Qur'an says that Muslims should repel evil with good.
- Ghaffar Khan claimed that peace and righteousness are the Prophet's weapons.

Now test yourself

TESTED

1 A person who objects to serving in the armed forces is called a:
   a) non-combatant
   b) pacifist
   c) conscientious objector
   d) Humanist
2 The belief that a country should have strong armed forces and be prepared to use them aggressively is known as:
   a) fascism
   b) militarism
   c) imperialism
   d) warmongering
3 The Sermon on the Mount is:
   a) Jesus' teaching on war
   b) Jesus' teaching on peace
   c) Jesus' description of Christian living
   d) Jesus' teaching on sharing with others
4 Non-violent opposition to authority is known as:
   a) pacifism
   b) protest movements
   c) passive resistance
   d) solidarity

Activities

Complete the answers to these questions:

1 Outline three features from the history of pacifism.

Pacifism began in the Roman Empire when several Roman writers wrote books against war. During the late nineteenth century, peace groups were formed and international peace congresses were held to promote pacifism and the end of war.

Following the development of nuclear weapons, groups such as .... campaigned against war.

2 Explain two reasons why some Muslims are pacifists. In your answer you must refer to a source of wisdom and authority.

Some Muslims are pacifists because of the bad effects of war and the teachings of the Qur'an which say that Muslims should fight evil with good. For example, Surah 5 records that Moses and Aaron refused to fight the Israelites who had rebelled against God and instead separated themselves from them. The Qur'an also says that ....

Exam support

You might be asked to evaluate a statement such as:

Pacifism and religion should go hand in hand.

The table below might help you answer such a question.

Arguments for	Arguments against
Jesus said that if Christians are hit on the right cheek they should turn and offer the left, meaning Christians should love their enemies.	The Qur'an says that Muslims must fight if they are attacked.
The Qur'an says that Muslims should fight evil with good.	Muhammad fought in wars.
Muhammad said that 'war is a deception'.	There are many hadith from Muhammad saying Muslims should fight in Just Wars.
Jesus said that Christians should love their enemies.	The Qur'an says that Muslims dying in a Just War will go straight to heaven.

Topic 2.4.5 Just War theory

REVISED

The Just War theory says that a war is just if the cause of the war is just and the war is fought using just methods.

Islam attitudes to Just War theory

REVISED

Islam says that a war is just if it:

- is fought for a just cause (either Islam is being attacked, or people are suffering a great injustice or in self-defence)
- is a **last resort** – all possible non-violent methods of solving the problem must have been tried
- is authorised and led by a Muslim authority
- is fought in such a way as to cause the minimum amount of suffering
- ensures that innocent civilians, especially the old, the young and women, are not deliberately attacked
- ends as soon as the enemy lays down their arms.

Most Muslims would agree that if a war fulfils these conditions, then a Muslim must fight in it because:

- the Qur'an says that Muslims must fight if they are attacked
- Muhammad is the great example for Muslims in how to live and he fought in wars
- Muhammad made many statements about war which say that Muslims must fight in Just Wars
- The Qur'an says that anyone who dies fighting in a Just War will go straight to heaven.

Modern weapons make it almost impossible to ensure **proportional methods** are used and for some Muslims this makes it virtually impossible to fight a just war and so they are against wars.

Other Muslims use ethical theories like Situation Ethics to determine whether a war is just. This would involve looking at the circumstances of the war to try to determine whether not fighting the war would be more unjust than fighting it. If they decide that the cause of the war is just because it meets the requirements of 'Just War theory' listed above, then they would consider a modern war to be a just war. It is generally considered just for a country to defend itself against attack by an **aggressor**.

Divergent Muslim attitudes to Just War

Some Muslims believe that a Just War is the lesser ***jihad*** and so all good Muslims should fight in it because it is part of a Muslim's struggle in the cause of God.

Some Muslims think that the only type of war that can be considered a lesser *jihad* is one that is being fought to defend a Muslim country from being attacked by a non-Muslim who wants to destroy Islam.

Some Muslims believe a lesser *jihad* Just War can be fought if the beliefs or practices of Islam are under threat, for example if a country banned *halal* methods of slaughtering animals.

Aggressor – someone who attacks without being provoked

Jihad – striving in the way of God

Last resort – after all other methods have been tried

Proportional methods – using weapons of the same factor as those used against you

Sources of wisdom and authority

- The Qur'an says that Muslims should fight in self-defence, but never be the aggressor.
- The Qur'an says that Muslims should fight to protect the innocent and should never harm women, children or the elderly.

Now test yourself

TESTED

1 An aggressor is:
   a) someone who attacks
   b) someone who attacks without being provoked
   c) someone who attacks after being provoked
   d) someone who kills indiscriminately
2 Last resort means:
   a) someone's final resting place
   b) after everything possible has been done
   c) after all other methods have been tried
   d) the last town on a road
3 Proportional methods means:
   a) using similar weapons to your opponents
   b) using weapons of the same factor as those used against you
   c) using superior weapons to those of your opponents
   d) using weapons in self-defence
4 *Jihad* means:
   a) fighting in a holy war
   b) fighting in a Muslim army
   c) striving in the way of God
   d) striving to fight evil

Activities

Complete the answers to these questions:

1 Outline three conditions necessary for a war to be called a Just War.

For a war to be considered just, it must be fought with the authority of the United Nations. It must be fought with the intention of restoring peace. Thirdly ....

2 Explain two reasons why Muslims will fight in a Just War. In your answer you must refer to a source of wisdom and authority.

Muhammad is the great example for Muslims in how to live and he fought in wars and made many statements (hadith) about war which say that Muslims must fight in Just Wars.

Another reason is that the Qur'an says that ....

Exam support

You might be asked to evaluate a statement such as:

Religious people should never fight in wars.

The table below might help you answer such a question.

Arguments for	Arguments against
Jesus said religious people should love their enemies and turn the other cheek.	The Qur'an says that Muslims must fight if they are attacked and Muslims believe the Qur'an is the word of God.
Surah 23 says that Muslims should fight evil with good.	Muhammad is the great example for Muslims in how to live and he fought in wars.
Religious people should never harm the innocent and the innocent are bound to be harmed in modern wars.	There are many hadith from Muhammad which say that Muslims must fight in Just Wars.
Religious people should always try to solve a situation peacefully without having to go to war.	The Qur'an says that anyone who dies fighting in a Just War will go straight to heaven.

Topic 2.4.6 Holy War

REVISED

A Holy War is a war which:

- is fought to achieve a religious goal
- is authorised by a religious leader
- promises a spiritual reward for those who fight in the war.

For example, the **crusades** in the eleventh century, were called by Pope to free the Holy Land from Muslim invaders. The Pope promised that any who died on the crusade would have their sins forgiven and would go straight to heaven.

Crusade – a war fought for a religious or moral purpose

Harb al-Muqadis – Muslim Holy War

Holy Wars often have terrible effects. Historians suggest that at least 1 million (and possibly as many as 3 million) people were killed in the Crusades. The sixteenth-century French Wars of Religion fought between Catholics and Protestants had between 2 and 3 million casualties. The Thirty Years War, fought in seventeenth-century Europe between Catholics and Protestants, had at least 3 million casualties and possibly up to 11 million. The United Nations estimates there to have been more than 250,000 casualties in the current Syrian civil war between Shi'a and Sunni Muslims.

Muslim teachings about war and peace

Holy War is known as **Harb al-Muqadis** in Islam. According to the Shari'ah, a Holy War can be fought to:

- defend Islam
- strengthen Islam
- protect the freedom of Muslims to practise their faith
- protect Muslims against attack
- put right a wrong.

Any Holy War would be regarded as a lesser *jihad* because it would be part of the struggle to defend Islam and make the world the abode of peace.

However, Islamic lawyers today believe that a Holy War can only be so called if it:

- is against an aggressor which threatens Islam
- is a last resort
- has been authorised and led by a religious leader chosen by the whole Muslim community
- only includes soldiers who are faithful Muslims, well-versed in the teachings of Islam.

If a Holy War fulfils these conditions then a Muslim must fight in it because the Qur'an says that Muslims must fight if they are attacked. Muhammad is the great example for Muslims about how to live and although he fought in wars, the hadith from Muhammad about war show how it must be limited to Holy and/or Just War.

Sources of wisdom and authority

- The Qur'an says that truly religious people will be prepared to fight in the cause of God.
- There is a hadith which says Muhammad said, 'Do not kill any child, any woman, or any elder or sick person.'

Non-religious attitudes to Holy War

Both atheists and Humanists believe there is no God and so religion is completely misguided and the truth about life is to be found in reason and science. Therefore, they believe that to fight a war based on religious ideas and in response to the orders of a religious leader is not only irrational, but also indefensible.

Now test yourself

TESTED

1 A crusade is:
  a) a war fought for a religious or moral purpose
  b) a war against another religion
  c) a Just War
  d) a war against Muslims
2 Sayings of the Prophet Muhammad are called:
  a) *haram*
  b) *halal*
  c) hadith
  d) *hadd*
3 Harb al-muqadis means:
  a) Muslim Just War theory
  b) that which is lawful for Muslims
  c) Muslim Holy War
  d) that which is forbidden for Muslims
4 'Faithful Muslims' are defined as:
  a) Muslims who are religious
  b) Shi'a Muslims
  c) Sunni Muslims
  d) Muslims who practise all the pillars or Acts and follow the Shari'ah

Activities

Complete the answers to these questions:

1 Outline three requirements for a war to be a Holy War.

One requirement is that the war must be fought to attain a religious goal. Another requirement is that it must be authorised by a religious leader. A third requirement is ....

....

2 Explain two reasons why Muslims might regard a war as a Holy War. In your answer you must refer to a source of wisdom and authority.

Muslims might regard a war as a Holy War if those fighting in the war are good Muslims, because the Qur'an says that truly religious people will be prepared to fight in the cause of God.

Muslims would also regard a war as a Holy War if it had been authorised and led by ....

....

Exam support

You might be asked to evaluate a statement such as: *No war should ever be called holy.*

The table below might help you answer such a question.

Arguments for	Arguments against
No war can be called holy because war involves killing people, which is forbidden in both Islam and Christianity.	According to the Shari'ah, a Holy War can be fought to defend Islam.
Wars are decided by humans who have no way of knowing whether or not God wants war.	A Holy War can be fought to strengthen Islam.
According to a hadith, 'Jaber reported that the Messenger of Allah said, "War is a deception."'	Holy War is justified to protect the freedom of Muslims to practise their faith and against attack.
Islam says a Holy War must be authorised and led by a religious leader chosen by the whole Muslim community; this cannot be done in the modern world.	Holy War is acceptable provided the soldiers are faithful Muslims and it is led by a good Muslim chosen by the Muslim community.

Topic 2.4.7 Weapons of mass destruction

REVISED

Weapons of mass destruction (WMD) can destroy large areas and/or large numbers of people.

Benefits of WMD

- When two countries have nuclear weapons, they will hesitate to attack each other because the other country could destroy them. This is known as **mutually assured destruction (MAD)**.
- Biological and chemical weapons can be used to destroy an enemy while leaving the infrastructure (buildings, roads and bridges, etc.) to be used by the attacker, who can be protected by protective clothing.

Problems of WMD

- Weapons of mass destruction deliberately target innocent civilians.
- The immense power of nuclear weapons means that any war fought using these weapons would threaten the world with extinction.
- Chemical and biological weapons are difficult to deliver effectively and the effects can only be guessed at.

Muslim attitudes to WMD

Islamic teachings make it difficult for Muslims to use WMD because a Muslim Just War must:

- avoid killing innocent civilians (especially the old, the young and women), but weapons of mass destruction deliberately target civilians
- use weapons proportional to the cause and this can never be the case with WMD, as they could destroy the world as we know it
- be fought in such a way as to cause the minimum amount of suffering, but WMD deliberately cause mass suffering
- end as soon as the enemy lays down their arms, but the enemy would have no chance to do this if WMD were used against them.

The spiritual leader of Iran, Ayatollah Khamenei, condemned the use of WMD by Muslims, but most Muslims accept that they can be held by a Muslim country to deter enemies.

Non-religious attitudes to WMD

Most Humanists and some atheists are against possessing WMD because their destructive power is totally against the basic Humanist belief of 'finding meaning, beauty and joy in the one life we have'. Humanists believe that this life and this earth is all we have as they do not believe in God and an afterlife in heaven. Consequently, they do not think it is right to contemplate the use of weapons which could destroy life on the planet.

Other atheists use the ethical principle of Utilitarianism to argue that it is acceptable for a country to possess WMD as self-defence, because the concept of MAD means possessing nuclear weapons will prevent attacks from other countries. This ensures world peace and 'bringing about the greatest happiness to the greatest number of people'.

Biological weapons – weapons that make use of some kind of virus or disease to infect millions of people

Chemical weapons – weapons that use chemicals such as nerve and blood agents to kill or disable enemies

Mutually assured destruction (MAD) – a strategy of stockpiling nuclear weapons by two or more opposing sides to deter the opposition from beginning nuclear strikes

Nuclear weapons – devices that explode through a nuclear reaction releasing a huge amount of energy

Sources of wisdom and authority

- There is a hadith which says 'Muhammad said, "Muslim wars must never involve killing children, women or the elderly and must not destroy the environment."'
- In October 2015, the spiritual leader of Iran, Ayatollah Khamenei said, 'Muslims are against any production of weapons of mass destruction in any form.'

Now test yourself

TESTED

1 Weapons that make use of a virus or disease to infect millions of people are called:
   a) nuclear weapons
   b) ballistic weapons
   c) biological weapons
   d) chemical weapons

2 Weapons which use nerve and blood agents to kill or disable enemies are:
   a) nuclear weapons
   b) ballistic weapons
   c) biological weapons
   d) chemical weapons

3 Weapons which use atomic power to kill enemies and destroy their property are:
   a) nuclear weapons
   b) ballistic weapons
   c) biological weapons
   d) chemical weapons

4 MAD stands for:
   a) missiles carrying atomic destruction
   b) mutual atomic defence
   c) mutually assured destruction
   d) mutually assured defence

Activities

Complete the answers to these questions:

1 Outline three types of weapons of mass destruction.

Three types of mass destruction weapons are nuclear weapons, which are extremely powerful bombs that can kill large numbers of people; chemical weapons which cause death or injury through their chemical action and ....

2 Explain two reasons why Muslims might be against possessing weapons of mass destruction. In your answer you must refer to a source of wisdom and authority.

Muslim might be against possessing weapons of mass destruction because for Muslims, a Just War must avoid killing innocent civilians and damage to the environment. According to a hadith, Muhammad said, 'Muslim wars must never involve killing children, women or the elderly and must not destroy the environment'. However, weapons of mass destruction deliberately target civilians and will cause great harm to the environment.

Another reason is ....

Exam support

You might be asked to evaluate a statement such as:

Weapons of mass destruction might be dreadful, but having them keeps the peace.

The table below might help you answer such a question.

Arguments for	Arguments against
There have been no world wars since 1945 because the two main enemies (the USA and Russia) have nuclear weapons.	Possessing WMD is against the teachings of Islam because a Muslim Just War must avoid killing innocent people, whereas WMD deliberately target civilians.
If a country knows that another country has WMD, they will not attack because of the fear that those weapons will be used against them.	A Muslim Just War must use weapons proportional to the cause and this can never be the case with WMD as they could lead to the destruction of the world as we know it.
No country that has nuclear weapons has been attacked.	WMD will not keep the peace if an irrational person becomes the leader of a country that has such weapons.

Topic 2.4.8 Issues surrounding conflict

REVISED

This topic covers violence, war and terrorism. However, the main issues surrounding conflict in connection with war are covered in Topic 2.4.3.

- **Violence:** Conflict usually results in violence and most violence actually occurs in the home (one in four women are likely to experience **domestic violence**, for example). Crimes such as burglary, robbery, rape, assault, kidnap, extortion and drug rackets are likely to be committed with violence.
- **Terroism:** Terrorists attack civilians to intimidate the population and compel governments to do what the terrorist group wants, such as the 9/11 Twin Towers attacks in New York and the 7/7 attacks in London.

Muslim attitudes to violence

Islam is against people using violence, except when authorised by the state, because:

- Islamic society is based on the rule of law and mutual respect between the members of that society
- Islam teaches that all Muslims are members of the ***ummah*** and should have equal treatment and respect
- it is the duty of Muslims to protect the weak and innocent, not to attack them.

Islam prohibits terrorism because:

- the Prophet Muhammad said, 'Do not kill women or children or non-combatants and do not kill old people or religious people'
- throughout their history, Muslims never allowed the killing of civilians, even in the midst of wars such as the Crusades
- suicide is *haram* (forbidden) in Islam, so a suicide bomber is going against Islam by committing suicide as well as bringing harm to innocent victims.

Domestic violence – violence in the home, mainly men attacking their partners

Terrorism – criminal acts intended to provoke a state of terror in the public for political or religious purposes

Ummah – the Muslim community (brotherhood of Islam)

7/7 – the London bombings of 7 July 2005

9/11 – the attacks in the USA on 11 September 2001

How Muslims have worked to overcome these issues

The Muslim Council of Britain has opposed terrorism by:

- paying for adverts to condemn terror in the name of many UK Muslim groups
- initiating a national process to explore grassroots responses to terrorism
- working closely with Muslim communities and the police to develop a successful counter-terrorism policy.

North American Muslims have formed the group Muslims Against Terrorism to work with Muslim and Christian organisations. In India, over 70,000 imams signed a document condemning global terrorist activity, which stated that they do not consider groups like Islamic State to be true Islamic organisations.

Sources of wisdom and authority

- Prophet Muhammad said: 'Do not kill women or children or non-combatants and do not kill old people or religious people.'
- The leader of the Ahmadiyya Muslims said, '... no true religion, whatever its name, can sanction violence and bloodshed of innocent men, women and children in the name of God.'

Atheist and Humanist attitudes to conflict

Humanists and most atheists are opposed to violence and terrorism. They believe it can never be right to terrorise and inflict violence on a civilian population. No matter what the terrorist's goal, it can never justify the means (using methods such as violence).

Now test yourself

TESTED

1 Criminal acts intended to provoke a state of terror in the public for political or religious purposes are known as:
   a) fascism
   b) terrorism
   c) Nazism
   d) fundamentalism
2 The Muslim community or brotherhood of Islam is called the:
   a) *ummah*
   b) *Uthman*
   c) *Usul ad-Din*
   d) *Umayyad*
3 7/7 refers to:
   a) the Paris bombings of 2015
   b) the London bombings of 2005
   c) the Twin Tower attacks of 2001
   d) the Nairobi attacks of 1998
4 9/11 refers to:
   a) the Paris bombings of 2015
   b) the London bombings of 2005
   c) the Twin Tower attacks of 2001
   d) the Nairobi attacks of 1998

Activities

Complete the answers to these questions:

1 Outline three ways in which Muslims fight terrorism.

Muslims fight terrorism by paying for adverts to condemn terror in the name of UK Muslims. They have also initiated a national process to explore grassroots responses to terrorism. A third way is ....

....

2 Explain two reasons why Muslims oppose terrorism. In your answer you must refer to a source of wisdom and authority.

Muslims oppose terrorism because suicide is haram in Islam, so a suicide bomber is going against Islam by committing suicide as well as bringing harm to innocent people. Another reason for opposing terrorism is that Islam prohibits a Muslim from attacking innocent civilians. There is a hadith in which the Prophet Muhammad says ....

Exam support

You might be asked to evaluate a statement such as: *Religion should do more to stop violence and terrorism.*

The table below might help you answer such a question.

Arguments for	Arguments against
The 9/11 attack in 2001, when Al Qaeda crashed airliners into New York's Twin Towers, was carried out in the name of religion.	UK Muslims have initiated a national process to explore grassroots responses to terrorism.
The 7 July 2005 suicide bomb attacks in central London which killed 52 civilians and injured 700 were carried out in the name of religion.	UK Muslim leaders are working closely with Muslim communities and the police to develop a successful counter-terrorism policy.
The Paris bombings of 2015 which killed 130 people were carried out in the name of religion.	The Ahmadiyya Muslims have condemned any form of terrorism and co-operate with the police and Muslim communities to report any suspect activities within their communities.
Religious attitudes to women have been used to justify violence against women.	North American Muslims have formed the group Muslims Against Terrorism.

How to deal with the exam paper

When you go into the exam hall and find your seat, your exam paper should be face up on the desk. Before you are allowed to open the paper, you can complete the front cover. Your paper will be scanned and put onto a computer for examiners to mark separate questions without seeing your name, so make sure you:

- spell your name correctly. If there is not enough room for your full name, write initials.
- write your centre number in correctly (this will be on display in the exam hall).
- write your personal exam number correctly (you will receive this from your school before the exam).

It is important that you get all of these completely correct, otherwise someone else may get your mark and grade! Also, if you run out of space in the exam do not go into the margins; ask for an extra sheet of paper instead. The scanner does not pick up any writing in the margins.

When you are told to start, make a note of the time. You have 26 minutes per question.

There is no choice of questions, so it is best just to work through the paper so you make the best use of your time.

Part a) questions usually ask you to outline three facts

- If you can only think of one or two facts then don't worry. Write down what you can and simply leave a space to come back to at the end and go on to part b).
- You should not spend more than 4 minutes on this question.

Part b) questions ask for two reasons

- Don't panic if you can only think of one reason. Extend your first reason (that might gain you an extra mark), then leave a space and go on to part c).
- Try to use some specialist vocabulary (key terms).
- You should not spend more than 4 minutes on this question.

Part c) questions ask for two reasons plus a reference to a source of wisdom and authority

- You don't need to learn quotations off by heart.
- A general idea of the quotation plus identifying where it comes from (no need for specifics) should get you the mark.
- That means there is no need to quote, for example: 'There are two sacraments ordained of Christ our Lord in the Gospel; that is to say, Baptism and the Supper of the Lord' – the 39 Articles of the Church of England. All you need for a mark is: 'the 39 Articles of the Church of England say there are the only two sacraments.'
- On abortion all you would need are statements such as, 'The Catholic Catechism says that life begins at conception.'
- You won't need to use the following full quotation: 'Wives submit to your own husbands as you do to the Lord. For the husband is the head of the wife as Christ is the head of the Church, his body, of which he is the Saviour.' Ephesians 5. Instead, you can just say: 'St Paul said that the husband is the head of the wife and so the wife should submit to him.'
- Try to use some specialist vocabulary (key terms).
- You should not spend more than 6 minutes on this question.

Part d) questions ask you to evaluate a controversial statement about a topic

- Read the question carefully to see whether you need to refer to two different points of view among Christians (you could refer to Protestants and Catholics), or two different points of view among Muslims (you could refer to liberal and traditional). If the question asks you to refer to non-religious points of view, you should use a Christian or Muslim point of view and non-religious points of view.

- When you have decided how the question wants you to evaluate the statement, you need to analyse the validity of the arguments used by those who would agree with the statement (i.e. explain whether and why each reason is convincing).
- Next use the arguments used by people who disagree (i.e. explaining whether and why each reason is convincing) to criticise the arguments in favour of the statement.
- Look back at the reasons you have given and decide whether you think they show that and then make your thoughts into a reasoned judgement on the statement.
- Remember that sections 1 and 3 have an extra 3 marks for SPAG in the d) questions. So be extra careful with your spelling and punctuation (especially full stops and capital letters) when answering these questions.

Area 2 Section 3

Remember, you may be asked to compare Christian and Muslim worship in this section, and you will need to know that Christianity is the major religion of the UK and that Islam, Judaism, Hinduism, Sikhism and Buddhism are widely practised.

If you have any time left:

- check that you have answered every part of each question
- if you have left spaces because you were not sure what to answer, see if you can think of something to write in (empty spaces cannot get more than zero but some writing may get a mark)
- go through your answers to the part d) questions in Sections 1 and 3, checking the spelling and grammar and trying to add some extra specialist vocabulary (useful terms).

Notes

Notes